WITHDRAWN FROM
KA 0015437 7

VOCATIONAL GUIDANCE

Vocational Guidance
Theory and Practice

W. P. Gothard

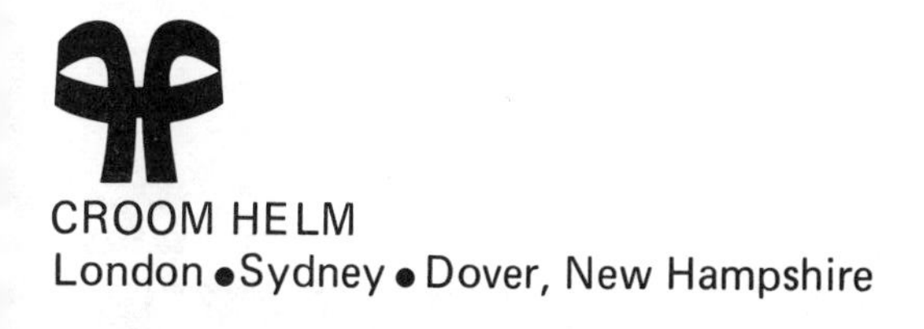
CROOM HELM
London • Sydney • Dover, New Hampshire

Croom Helm Ltd, Provident House,
Burrell Row, Beckenham, Kent BR3 1AT
Croom Helm Australia Pty Ltd, First Floor,
139 King Street, Sydney, NSW 2001, Australia

British Library Cataloguing in Publication Data

Gothard, W.P.
Vocational guidance: theory and practice.
1. Vocational guidance
I. Title
371.4'25 HF5381

ISBN 0-7099-1161-0

Croom Helm, 51 Washington Street,
Dover, New Hampshire 03820, USA

Library of Congress Cataloging in Publication Data

Gothard, W.P.
Vocational guidance.

Bibliography: p.
Includes index.
1. Vocational guidance. I. Title.
HF5381.G814 1985 371.4'25 84-23780
ISBN 0-7099-1161-0 (U.S.)

Printed and bound in Great Britain by
Biddles Ltd, Guildford and King's Lynn

CONTENTS

PREFACE

It is hoped that this book will be useful to a wide range of people involved in vocational guidance and counselling. The intention is to provide a wide ranging review of theory and practice in the hope that this will encourage readers to stop and think about some of their practices and then to read further in the extensive literature available. In many respects, this is an appropriate time to be looking at the theory and practice of vocational guidance as the whole concept of work is being re-examined. New developments, such as the Youth Training Scheme, are underway and inevitably the roles of those engaged in vocational guidance are changing. Flexibility and a willingness to adapt are qualities looked for amongst the working population today and this is certainly true of those working in the field of vocational guidance.

Chapter One

VOCATIONAL GUIDANCE IN CONTEXT

"A theory is a means of organising and interpreting all that is known concerning a related set of events". Hall and Lindzey.(1978)

Careers advisers are essentially practical people. Their role is much concerned with such practical matters as providing young people with information about occupations and, in some cases, helping them to find employment. Theory would seem to have little place and yet all careers advisers construct and apply their 'theory' of Occupational Choice, each working day. For most of them it is implicit, hardly conscious, but still it plays a central part in their role. If questioned, few careers advisers would associate their own particular style of helping with any particular theorist, but this would inevitably ignore the broad influence of much psychological and sociological writing this century, upon their actions. A basic understanding of the development of this writing will help the careers adviser to put his own work into a broader context.

Tracing the development of Occupational Choice Theory is best done against the background of the wider development of ideas about the nature of man and his place in society. It is necessary to look at early developments in the United States in order to understand the growth of vocational guidance in Britain. This may have been due to the fact that the U.S.A. has always been a more socially mobile society than our own and, at the beginning of this century, was experiencing very rapid social and economic change.

The very early practitioners such as Parsons were mainly interested in questions of social reform and the general welfare of citizens. Frank Parsons, educated as an engineer and a lawyer, worked as a college teacher and social worker before helping to establish the Vocation Bureau in

Boston, U.S.A. in 1908. Parsons died soon afterwards, in 1909, but his ideas had become established and have influenced the practice of Vocational Guidance to this day.

Parsons (1909) stated "First, a clear understanding of yourself, aptitudes, abilities, interests, resources, limitations and other qualities. Second, a knowledge of the requirements and conditions of success, advantages and disadvantage, compensation, opportunities and prospects in different lines of work. Third, true reasoning on the relations of these two groups of facts." This has remained the 'Conventional Wisdom' since 1908, forming the basis of the 'Talent Matching' approach, and only being challenged in more recent years by other theories of Occupational Choice.

Parsons went further than stating general principles. He set out a series of techniques, beginning with the collection of personal data, by means of a private interview at some length. "Ancestry, family, education, reading, experience, interests, aptitudes, abilities, limitations, resouces etc. are enquired into with a vigor and directness that are not possible in a written research." Various tests of sight and hearing might well be used, as well as an assessment of memory and general intelligence. He was also concerned with 'character analysis' during the interview. This involved careful observation of head shape, features, pose, voice, vitality etc. Parsons saw it as part of his work to advise interviewees on the 'value of voice culture' and the "economic value of the smile" and "if the manners are in any way objectionable or underdevloped, the boy should be frankly told and urged to correct his errors".

Occupational information was the basis of his second area of interest and he collected this for use with clients. For "the boy who is underdeveloped and inexperienced and shows no special aptitudes", he advised him to read about occupations and visit places of work and, if feasible, " try his hand at different kinds of work". Such was the influence of Parson's work, that in 1918 a report of the Commission on the reoganisation of Secondary Education (Dept. of the Interior) stated that

"Vocational Guidance, properly conceived,

> organizes schoolwork so that the pupil may be helped to discover his own capacities, aptitudes and interests, may himself learn about the character and conditions of occupational life and may himself arrive at an intelligent vocational decision."

Frank Parsons does not seem to have been much influenced by the psychological thinking of the time. His was essentially a pragmatic approach. However, there were psychologists who were his contemporaries, who did contribute to the theory and practice of vocational guidance. Their interest and contribution arose from their work in Industrial psychology. Hugo Munsterberg (1912) was possibly the leading figure in this field to apply himself to vocational guidance. Through his work on individual differences and their application to employment selection, he applied his findings to occupational choice. He stated that "a vocation should be chosen only when one understands the interrelationships within a given occupation of the motive factor, the knowledge factor and the ability factor."

At the same time, there was a growing interest in matching "man and machine", and this was personified in the work of F.W. Taylor and F.B. Gilbreth. Taylor has become identified with the notion of 'scientific management' and with it, a drive to reduce inefficiency. In this process, work was to be studied closely and, as a result, the abilities required to perform certain tasks became more clearly identified. This gradually initiated a concern for better selection methods to produce better equipped workers.

As we have seen, Industrial Psychologists were becoming increasingly interested in this field, an interest that was stimulated by the First World War. In a sense, this is where the earliest British interest in Vocational Guidance arises. Cyril Burt joined C.S. Myers at the newly founded National Institute of Industrial Psychology in 1921 and initiated a programme of research, which later involved Alec Rodger and carried on until the Second World War. This research focussed on the usefulness of psychometric information in guidance and on the need for clearer and more extensive knowledge of occupations. Indeed, psychological testing can be seen as the common meeting point for personnel selection and vocational guidance at this time.

Despite the work of N.I.I.P., the Juvenile Employment Service did not readily take to psychological testing. Indeed, Birmingham was the only education authority that became extensively involved, and in 1944, they published a report stating that "the adoption of scientific methods in vocational guidance improves considerably the advice that can be given to children leaving school". This statement was based upon a study of 1600 children, some of whom were followed up for as long as four years after starting work. The study claimed to show that those guided by tests made sounder choices. It is interesting to note that the children were medically examined, a home visit was conducted, and six tests were administered. A choice of employment conference was arranged and prior to this, the head teacher, the teacher responsible for testing and the juvenile employment officer met to decide upon the vocational guidance to be given.

Psychological testing has remained a minor activity within the mainstream of British vocational guidance practice. This is despite the introduction of D.E.V.A.T., (Dept. of Employment Vocational Assessment Test Battery), in 1971. Careers Officers were trained to use the tests but by 1977 less than a quarter of all the pupils were being tested. However, the talent matching model, initiated by Parsons, has persisted over time. The notion that vocational guidance was the search for a close match between the assets of the client and the known requirements of a range of occupations remained the predominant practice until the 1970's. The Seven Point Plan devised by Alec Rodger in 1930 formed the basis for this practice. Rodger played a leading role in the training of Youth Employment Officers in the two decades following the 1948 Employment and Training Act.

Change in professional practice is difficult to monitor accurately, but Roberts (1971) claims that in 1969, in the course of a research project amongst youth employment officers, he "discovered that the idiom of the developmental theories had become a conventional wisdom". He states that many youth employment officers were critical of earlier directive methods and were keen to develop careers education in schools. This coincided with a move to increase the number of careers teachers in schools and to make the Youth Employment Service more education based, and rather less concerned with placing youngsters in employment. About this time, counsellor training was becoming established at the Universities of Reading and Keele, and with it, the work of counselling theorists such as Carl Rogers were becoming more widely read. However, it is the work of Ginzberg et al (1951) and Super (1957) that Roberts associated directly with this move to a developmental method of practice. It was also in 1966 that Daws first published his paper "A Good Start in Life", having helped establish the Vocational Guidance Research Unit, a year earlier. Looking back, it is clear that changes were taking place that were to be important for the future of vocational guidance in the U.K.

When considering change in professional practice, it is as well to remember the broader social and economic context in which it was happening. The sixties was a period of growing prosperity, with an economy that was demanding a regular supply of young labour. It was a time of new youth sub cultures and there were also important changes in secondary education with the growing number of comprehensives. All those factors contributed to a view of vocational guidance that laid emphasis on individual self development and choice. It was in this context that Daws (1972) made five basic recommendations for vocational guidance practice that have been important in the intervening period. The recommendations were:

1.) Vocational Development - Daws makes a plea for earlier vocational guidance in schools. He links this with educational decisions that have to be made well before the school leaving age. Indeed, with comprehensive education potentially offering a greater educational opportunity, a good case for an increasingly important role for vocational guidance can be made. Using Super's life stages (1953), Daws promotes the case for an extended service available to young people at school.

2.) Counselling - the adequacy of 'talent matching' is questioned, and the notion that self discovery and personal growth are important goals in vocational guidance is supported. Daws points out the importance of Carl Rogers's ideas on counselling in the United States, and states that his emphasis on enabling the client to make decisions for himself is much more productive in the long term. Counselling also stresses the importance of seeing the individual as a whole and not purely in terms of vocational decisions or choices. When Daws comes to define the tasks of vocational guidance, he describes them in non-directive counselling terms.

3.) Needs and Values - the matching of person and job is not disputed, but "what is unacceptable is a biased matching conception which is limited to to talent matching or the weighing of labour market assets". Job satisfaction is not just being able to do the job adequately, and Daws accuses the seven point plan of being an instrument "derived from the employer's point of view". He says it also does not give enough attention to the role of training or motivation in achieving success at work. In effect, the seven point plan is a narrow, functional way of looking at people and judging their occupational fitness. It derives from an earlier age, when getting a job and doing it competently was sufficient. Daws is making a plea for the work of people like Elton Mayo to be taken into consideration rather than the purely mechanistic view of man promoted by F.W. Taylor. Mayo helped to begin the 'Human Relations' movement in industrial psychology which pointed out the key importance of working groups and interpersonal relations at work. Therefore, needs and values have a crucial role to play in vocational counselling. It is also necessary to consider how people feel, as well as how they think and perform physically.

4.) After Care - Having made a case for earlier preparation for occupational choice, Daws also stresses the need to provide a support service for young people, once they have left education. The "review of progress" does not do this adequately and there is a need for the Youth Employment Service to be in touch with the employers of young people on a regular basis advising them on matters such as induction and training, which would also give the opportunity to find out how youngsters were progressing. (It is ironic that this sort of activity has only become practiced on a wide scale with the advent of special schemes to combat unemployment, as well as the provision of special posts (U.S.C.O.s) to deal solely with those who have left school. By October 1982, there were 1060 posts, out of a total of 6,330 Careers Service staff).

5.) Guidance Teams - there is an important need to create a team approach (Albermarle Report 1965). The Youth Employment Officer should work closely with the Careers Teacher, who in turn will liaise with other members of the school staff, especially the Counsellor, if there is one. With increased pressure to help unemployed youngsters, the Careers Service, in recent years, has tended to concentrate less of its resources in schools. In some L.E.A.s, this has been made worse by a reduction in financial support for the Service. The overall concept of a guidance team has been steadily eroded because of this, and other cutbacks in the staffing of schools. In fact, the overall provision of vocational guidance has declined in the last few years, accentuated by the closure of Occupational Guidance Units, which clearly fulfilled an important need for adult guidance.

This chapter began by looking at the beginnings of vocational guidance and has briefly traced its development to the present. A more detailed examination of vocational guidance theory and practice will take place in the subsequent chapters. Before this is done, it is worthwhile to look at some of the concepts, or frames of reference that are fundamental to a consideration of occupational choice. Crites (1969) suggests that there are five sets of concepts that need to be considered. Firstly, how far is occupational choice the result of systematic behaviour as opposed to chance? Clearly the practice of vocational guidance is concerned with systematizing choice and there is an unspoken assumption that occupational choice ought to be planned and systematic. For instance, Trait and Factor Guidance is concerned with predicting occupational choice on the basis of the systematic investigation of the individual and then matching this profile to a likely occupation, which again will have been systematically investigated. As little as possible is left to chance, luck or intuition. How far this can be true in reality is open to question, but it is true to say that all vocational guidance or counselling is trying to reduce the degree of chance in occupational choice in order to increase the likelihood of the individual making a more satisfactory choice of job.

Crites has raised the question of conscious and unconscious behaviour. Again, trait and factor theory and practice is based firmly on the principle that occupational choice is rational, cognitive and conscious. At the other extreme are those psychoanalytic writers who produced work on this subject. Super (1957) proposed that self awareness is a developmental process and therefore that occupational choice is likely to become more conscious and satisfactory as the individual moves through the various life stages. There is an inherent difficulty in establishing how far occupational choice is, or is not based on conscious behaviour. Those working in vocational guidance have subscribed to the view that it is a result of conscious, and therefore more easily accessible behaviour. Psychoanalysis is unlikely to change this prevailng position. The question of how far occupational choice is rational or emotional is perhaps more productive. Certainly, the early influential figures in vocational guidance, such as Parsons and Williamson laid great emphasis on reasoning, thinking through problems and rationality in general. This was as opposed to behaviour that was based on feelings, attitudes and needs. Barry and Wolf (1962) are highly critical of vocational guidance based on reasoned choice. They maintain that this is impossible and also raise the question of who decides whether a choice is realistic or not. Trait and factor guidance is based on the premise that the interviewer is ultimately the expert and that his opinion of what is realistic or not is the most valid view. Such an approach is difficult to support on a number of grounds, especially when clients disprove the forecasts of those in vocational guidance, by achieving the 'unrealistic'.

Is occupational choice a compromise or a synthesis? Ginzberg et al (1951) saw it in terms of a compromise, where the individual weighs up the possible satisfactions of a job. Super (1956) maintains that the process of choice takes place over a long period, and is a gradual synthesis of significant factors. This question clearly has significance for the last set of concepts; event or process. Trait and factor guidance has been based on the notion that occupational choice is an event, a decision that has to take place. Youngsters are confronted with the need to make a choice when they are about to leave full-time education. For some, this is a "crisis" because they are unable to decide; for others the choice is much easier, but in either case, by skilful matching, each youngster can be advised as to a suitable job. The developmentalists, like Super, see occupational choice in terms of process, the formation of a self concept, and the movement through a series of life stages before occupational choice is finally established.

In conclusion, it is worth looking critically at some of the underlying assumptions of vocational guidance. Warnath (1979) claims that one of these assumptions sees individuals who have adequate information, guidance and motivation, being able to find a job that fits them satisfactorily and also satisfies them. There is an underlying feeling that each job has something to offer and that there is someone who can do the job and get something worthwhile from it. He maintains that this loses sight of the fact that many jobs have been 'dehumanised' by technological change, whilst there has always been some sort of pressure on careers officers to fill existing jobs, even though those seeking work may have been over-qualified.

The Protestant work ethic is still very pervasive, but work can be seen as alienating, as well as satisfying. Ultimately, most work is concerned with fulfilling certain economic requirements, rather than giving pleasure to the individual, and thus for many, there is a conflict of interest. Warnath is critical of both vocational theorists and counsellors who, he says, "are engaged in a basically amoral activity, operating on the premise that the working world is just and is guided by rational principles in regard to those employed in work - despite the fact that the system within which those workers are engaged responds to factors quite unrelated to the welfare of the individual worker and can fulfill the needs of individuals only insofar as these needs support the needs of the organisation". What is certain is that those engaged in this field need to be aware of change, responsive to the impact of this change, and to be reminded, from time to time, that their first duty is to their clients, rather than to a particular economic system, government, or employer.

Chapter Two

PSYCHOLOGICAL EXPLANATIONS OF OCCUPATIONAL CHOICE

"There are many theories of vocational development and none of them is such that we could embrace it with any confidence" Kline (1975)

It is appropriate to begin by examining the contribution that psychology has made to our understanding of occupational choice as this is the discipline that has paid most attention to the theory and the practice of vocational guidance. Chapter One has outlined the history of vocational guidance, and the early influence of industrial psychology is clearly apparent. Thus, it was inevitable that different aptitudes should become the main focus of vocational psychologists in the first half of this century.

1.) Trait and Factor Theory

Differential psychology is concerned with the examination of individual differences in terms of traits and factors. In the United States, the leading proponents of this approach were D.G. Paterson and E.G. Williamson, both of the University of Minnesota. Whilst Paterson worked in the Employment Stabilisation Research Institute, developing various aptitude tests for use in vocational guidance, it was Williamson who promoted the trait and factor theory, and helped to establish its widespread practice. The theory is based on the following premises:

a.) Individuals are organised in terms of a unique pattern of capabilities and potentialities (traits).

b.) These traits are correlated with the requirements of different jobs.

c.) Testing is the best means of predicting

future job success.

d.) Each individual attempts to identify his own traits in order to find a way of working and living which will enable him to use his capabilities effectively.

Williamson laid great emphasis on man as a rational being, who once possessing adequate information about himself is then capable of making a wise choice. The counsellor uses a selection of tests and other devices to help his client to put his aptitudes, interests and personality into some sort of occupational context. Alec Rodger (1971) developed a 'trait and factor' working framework, the Seven Point Plan, which became widely adopted in the U.K. The plan stated that those engaged in vocational guidance need to assemble a profile of information, for each individual, based on the following seven areas.

1.) Physical Make-up,
2.) Attainments.
3.) General Intelligence.
4.) Special Aptitudes.
5.) Interests.
6.) Disposition.
7.) Circumstances.

Rodger describes the plan as a "simple but scientifically defensible assessment system", applicable to vocational guidance or employment selection. The plan is based on "old fashioned dichotomies familiar to psychologists", external influences described as circumstances and internal influences called attributes.

The Seven Point Plan bears closer examination as it enshrines much of the 'trait and factor' theory, and has played an important part in vocational guidance practice in this country. Rodger posed two questions about physical make-up. Firstly, has the interviewee any defects of health or physique that may be of occupational importance? This is clearly a sensible and important area to explore, although it may not be easy for the adviser to state the occupational signficance of certain defects very definitely. Rodger makes the point that some employers are unwilling to 'risk' employing those with handicaps, although there is evidence to show that in many cases, these handicaps can be successfully overcome at work. Secondly, how agreeable is his appearance, his bearing, and his speech? Rodger talks of averages of agreeability for age, sex and education, but really fails to acknowledge the difficulties inherent in this question. The issues raised are many, and centre around the subjectivity, values and prejudices of the interviewer, as well as the requirements of employers; many of which may be hidden, but still very important, e.g. no long hair, no black skin, must be "well spoken" etc.

Attainments relate to educational achievements and those outside the "narrow classroom sense". This information can be obtained from the interviewee, the school and parents. Rodger also includes occupational training and experience for those already at work. General intelligence means general intellectual capacity and Rodger advocates the use of tests to establish this, whilst using the interview to explore how far this intelligence is normally used. Special Aptitudes cover mechanical, manual dexterity, facility in the use of words or figures, talent for drawing or music. Tests can be used to measure some of these aptitudes, although Rodger warns against too much occupational significance being attached to these special aptitudes. General intelligence is more important.

To what extent are his interests intellectual, practical constructional, physically active, social, artistic? Rodger says that interests have to be treated cautiously as they may be short lived, unsoundly based, and not relate to actual accomplishments. Indeed, he asks whether drives such as doing good or making money are more relevant, but concludes that there is a five fold classification of occupations:

1.) Those with intellectual processes, e.g. clerical work.

2.) Those of mainly practical constructional type,e.g. engineering.

3.) Those of mainly physically active type, e.g. farming.

4.) Those involving, essentially, some relationship with other people, e.g. sales.

5.) Those of mainly artistic kind.

Disposition has to do with personality, temperament and character, although Rodger suggests that it is more useful to pose four questions about disposition. How acceptable does he make himself to other people? Does he influence others? Is he steady and dependable? Is he self reliant? These relate to the most frequently taken into account qualities used by a group of 'experienced psychologists' in an extensive study of disposition. Whilst accepting their importance in occupational terms, there are two criticisms to level at Rodger's classification. Firstly, he says nothing about the subjectivity and changeability of these elements of disposition. Secondly, there is no mention of values, which will inevitably play an important part in occupational choice. Interestingly, Rodger doesn't mention personality tests, although these have been available for many years, and have been used by some employers for selection purposes. It may be that he didn't see these tests being readily available to those engaged in vocational guidance.

Daws (1972), commenting on the 'trait and factor' approach, says that it follows inevitably that there will be a specialist to give information, advice and make recommendations. The most appropriate time will be just before the client has to commit himself to an occupational choice, for then the necessary profile of the client will be most up to date. Rodger had some comments to make on the style of the interview based on the Seven Point Plan. He talks of persuading the subject to accept his suggestions, of making somewhat biased statements about the subject's occupational choices, that are clearly unsuitable, and of stressing the advantages of occupations for which the subject appears to be well fitted. He does not advocate forcing the subject to accept suggestions, but the the interviewer should aim to make the subject's conclusions the same as his conclusions. To do this, he should adopt a fairly authoritative manner. At the end of this process, he should be "careful to avoid encouraging and excessively dependent attitude"!

These remarks, made by Rodger, do sum up a number of important features of 'trait and factor' practice. The interviewer is seen as an authority figure, processing specialist knowledge that entitles him to make statements, diagnose, prescribe and persuade the 'subject'. The use of the term 'subject' is significant because it does imply a passivity on the part of the client. A subject is something to be studied, measured and directed. The analogy with medicine is clear in the 'trait and factor' approach. The interviewer, like the doctor, has access to skills and knowledge that are denied to the subject. The subject has to rely on the superior judgement of the interviewer to find a solution to his problem.

Weinrach (1979) has questioned a number of underlying assumptions of 'trait and factor' theory. Testing used by employers and vocational guidance is crucial, and yet there is increasing evidence to question their accuracy, and general applicability. Interest and personalty testing also have their limitations. The emphasis on 'once and for all' choice does suggest a static view of the client, which is less and less true to a rapidly changing world. Likewise, the notion of finding a "close match" of person and job is less and less likely in a depressed economy. Finally, the degree of dependency that this approach supports is both unsatisfactory for the client's future needs and unlikely to be very helpful in arriving at a choice that is primarily his, and not the interviewer's.

It is important to say something about rationality. Williamson laid great emphasis on the need for rationality in vocational guidance and by implication,in employer selection methods. This denies two crucial points. Clients may attempt to make rational choices, but will still be heavily influenced by the irrational, and the intuitive; in other words, their feelings. Too much emphasis on the cognitive masks the importance of feelings in choice, and no amount of 'scientific' vocational guidance is going to remove that. The other weakness lies in the assumption that employers are mainly rational in their selection methods and therefore once a "rational' occupational choice (assessment) has been made, this can be successfully 'matched' by the chosen employer, when employing the client. In practice, employers use non-rational factors as part of their selection methods, e.g. sex, colour, type of school, religion, hair style, etc.

PSYCHOLOGICAL EXPLANATIONS OF OCCUPATIONAL CHOICE

Summary

Bearing in mind the limitations of 'trait and factor' theory and practice, why has it persisted for so long? Inevitably there are various answers to this question. Psychometrics have had a long and influential history and, once vocational guidance had become wedded to differential psychology, it became very difficult to move in other directions. This was especially true as psychological testing was being enthusiastically and extensively used in other areas of education. The 'relevance' of this approach seemed to be borne out by similar practices of employers, which gave it credibility in relation to the needs of the labour market. Finally, there is an understandable attraction to a theory which offers hope of a neat match between jobs that are waiting to be filled and people who want jobs.

2.) Personality

a.) Anne Roe, an American clinical psychlogist, was one of the first to propose a theory of career choice based upon personality development. Between 1951 and 1953, she published a series of articles based on the study of personality differences of five scientists and social scientists. Out of this developed a more formal theoretical statement (Roe 1957, Roe and Siegelman, 1964). Fundamental to her thinking is a basic assumption of the importance of early childhood experiences, the canalization of psychic energy and the part that needs play in occupational choice. Roe makes a number of general statements which are difficult to test empirically. For instance, the view that individual's expend psychic energy in a way that is not exactly under their control, and that this is influential in the development of the individual's abilities.

She utilised Maslow's hierarchy of needs (1954) to help explain the part that needs play in occupational choice. Basic needs are patterned on the basis of childhood experiences. Three propositions are made:-

1.) Needs that are routinely satisfied do not become unconscious motivators.

2.) Higher order needs (such as need for

beauty) will disappear entirely if they are only rarely satisfied, as lower order needs (such as safety) will be predominant.

3.) Needs that are satisfied, after an unusual delay, will become unconscious motivators, under certain conditions.

Roe classifies child rearing into three categories, and lays emphasis on the attitudes toward the child. Firstly, there is a range of emotional concentration on the child from over protection to over demandingness. Secondly, avoidance of the child takes the form of two extremes of emotional rejection and neglect. Thirdly, there is acceptance of the child, either in a casual manner by default or by loving non-interference. Arising from this initial relationship, with parents, is an occupational classification based upon an alienation towards or away from persons. There are four groups towards persons - Service, Business, Organization, General cultural, arts and entertainment. The other three groups are not towards persons - technology, outdoor and science. Roe includes six levels of occupation - unskilled, semi-skilled, skilled, semi-professional, and two levels of professional and managerial.

Osipow (1973) states that the theory deals with every important aspect of vocational selection. Emphasis is on the early environment, and the influence that this has on needs development is made clear. The intensity of the needs will determine motivation. Barry and Wolf (1962) applaud the application of Maslow's hierarchy, seeing this as introducing a dynamic approach to vocational guidance. Super (1981) is more critical and questions the theory for making the error that early childhood development determines later career patterns. Roe's theory has stimulated a good deal of research which has not, for the most part, supported it. Certainly it has played no part in the practice of vocational guidance.

b.) There is a strong element of the psychoanalytic in Roe's work, and it is worth looking at some other contributions to the understanding of occupational choice, from this area of psychology. Freud saw work as an important outlet for man (but not woman) to sublimate his wishes and impulses. Subsequently, a number of other writers have directed their attention to occupational choice, although it has been seen more as a by-product of personality development, and thus of secondary interest. However, Bordin, Nachmann and Segal (1963) produced a 'framework for vocational development'. This stated that

1.) The earliest psychological and physiological processes are linked to later more complex activities in adult life.

2.) Instinctive sources of gratification are the same for adult behaviour, as for infancy.

3.) Needs are determined in the first six years, although there may be some later modifications.

4.) These needs determine the occupation sought.

5.) The theory applies to all ages and levels of work, except where freedom of choice is severely restricted, or where there is little or no gratification in the work.

6.) Work allows the sublimation of infantile impulses into socially acceptable behaviour.

7.) A lack of knowledge of occupations can result in a faulty choice.

8.) All jobs cluster around various psychoanalytic needs.

Kline (1975) also regards psychoanalytic theory as useful in understanding occupational choice: he suggests some relationship between oral fixation and occupation such as cooking and barrister; anal fixation and lawyers, archivists and accountancy; phallic fixation and firemen. However, although psychoanalytic thought may be of interest, it has not made any impact on theory building or upon vocational guidance in general.

c.) John Holland's work on vocational choice dates back to 1959, and has continued unabated since that time. Osipow (1973) describes his theory as based on career choices representing an extension of personality and that there is an attempt to implement personal behavioural styles in the context of work.

Holland's assumptions (1973) underlying his theory are

1.) "In our culture, most persons can be categorised as one of six types - realistic, investigative, artistic, social, enterprising or conventional".

2.) "There are six types of environments - realistic, investigative, artistic, social, enterprising or conventional". As people of the same type congregate, they help create an environment, typical of their particular type.

3.) "People search for environments that will let them exercise their skills and abilities, express their attitudes and values, and take on agreeable problems and roles".

4.) "A person's behaviour is determined by an interaction between his personality and the characteristics of his environment".

In addition, Holland refers to some other key concepts.

a.) Consistency - some types have more in common with other types. Figure 1 demonstrates the relationship between types. Correlations between the types are indicated.

b.) Differentiation - some people and some environments are much closer to one type, whilst other people and environments are much more a mixture of types.

c.) Congruence - there are degrees of fit between people and environments, e.g. a realistic type fits best into a realistic environment, and next best, into an investigative environment.

Figure 2.1

Relationships among Types

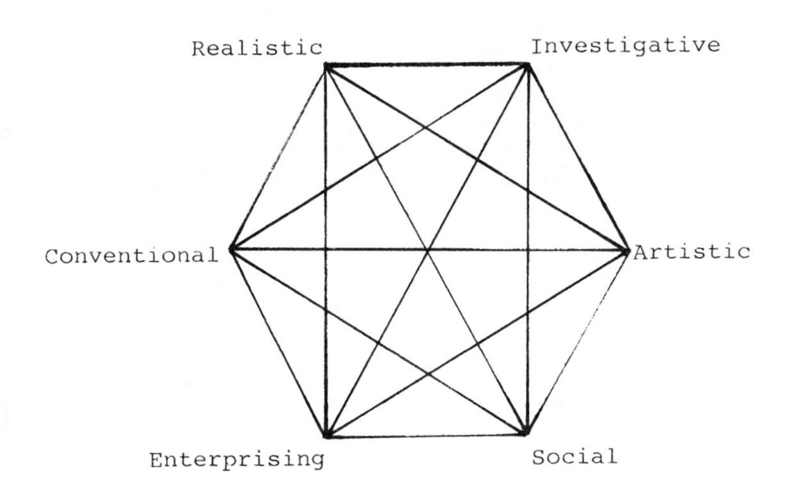

Holland describes his six personality types in some detail. He says that each is a model orientation based on "coping mechanisms, psychological needs and motives, self concepts, life history, vocational and educational goals, preferred occupational roles, aptitudes and intelligence".

Realistic - physically strong, unsociable, aggressive, lacks verbal skills, but has good motor coordination. Has conventional political and economic values. Examples of occupations - surveyor, car mechanic, plumbing, radio operator.

Investigative - needs to understand, likes thinking through problems, task orientated, has unconventional values and attitudes. Examples of occupations - geologist, editor of scientific journal, design engineer.

Social - sociable, responsible, religious, has verbal and interpersonal skills, prefers to solve problems through feelings. Examples of occupations - counsellor, social worker, speech therapist, teacher.

Conventional - conforming, likes well structured tasks, values, material possessions and status, prefers structured verbal and numerical activities and subordinate roles. Examples of occupations - bank clerk, statistician, quality controller.

Enterprising - uses verbal skills for selling, leading; likes ambiguous social tasks, great concern for power and status. Examples of occupations - T.V. producer, estate agent, buyer, hotel manager.

Artistic - tends to be introverted, rejects conventional values, but has high ideals. Avoids problems that are highly structured or require gross physical skills, has a need for individualistic expression. Examples of occupations - author, composer, stage director, commercial artist.

Holland states that a person's primary direction of choice is determined by the model type he most resembles, e.g. Investigative - scientist. However, individuals also have a secondary direction determined by the model type he most resembles, e.g. Investigative/Social - science teacher. This determines the choice of role within the environment. Holland also perceives the realistic and investigative types as more stable in their choices, whilst enterprising social and artistic types have higher aspirations. He also associates high educational aspirations with investigative, social, artistic, as opposed to realistic. Creativity is most associated with investigative and artistic.

Working environments are largely created by the typical characteristics of those working within them. There is a mutual attraction operating which can be seen when employers recruit in their "own image", and choose the sort of people who "will fit in". Likewise, applicants try and sense whether they can relate to fellow workers, when deciding whether to accept a job or not. Holland does point out that tasks and situations, and not just people, are important when it comes to choice. There is more sublety in Holland's types and environments than may appear at first sight. He perceives individuals in terms of a first, second and third type, and also states that work environments are made up of a combination of environmental models. Thus, a realistic environment for instance, may have elements of an investigative environment as well.

Holland, like Roe, emphasises early childhood development. He says that

> "the stable person probably had parents whose individual personality patterns are consistent both in themselves and in relation to the other parent's personality pattern...... In short, personal stability is the outcome of passing through a series of consistent environments that foster and strengthen one's ability to cope with the world in an integrated way".

Change does take place during peoples' lives, and the types most likely to change are Social, Enterprising, Conventional, Artistic, Investigative and Realistic, in that order.

Holland has always been interested in developing instruments for use in vocational guidance, arising from his research work. The Self Directed Search (1977), Occupations Finder (1977), and the Vocational Preference Inventory (1977) are the fruit of this interest. In addition, the Strong Campbell Vocational Interest Blank, (1977), and Bolle's quick job hunting map (1979) use his personality types. All these instruments will be considered in Chapter 6.

Holland's work has generated more interest in the United States, than any other theory of occupational choice. Not all this interest has been uncritical. Weinrach (1979) lists a number of weaknesses. For instance, Holland's model is sexist, although he does admit to a lack of data on women. This is true of the self directed search. In addition, his theory does not explain how people become the types they are, which can be regarded as a major shortcoming. Holland, by emphasising the value of the self directed search, plays down the need for individual help and counselling. This may well be 'cost effective' and therefore attractive in today's world, but it can also be seen as taking a risk that some will make uninformed and unsatisfactory choices which could have been avoided. Finally, Holland's theory does suggest a matching process which can be described as simplistic and static. Super (1981) feels that little of substance has really been verified in Holland's work.

3. <u>Developmental</u>

a.) Ginzberg et al (1951) are credited with being first to emphasise the developmental aspects of occupational choice. Their research was based on a small, unrepresentative sample and was conducted over a period of years, with a series of interviews. The conclusions were as follows

a) occupational choice is a process that takes place over six to ten years,

b) the process of decision making is irreversible,

c.) the crystallization of occupational choice inevitably has the quality of compromise.

Individuals move through three stages. Firstly, the fantasy period lasts until eleven and is based on needs and impulses. Secondly, the tentative period lasts until seventeen. Interests, abilities and values are used to make choices. During this period, interests predominate at first, but are then superceded by a concern for capacities. Values at fifteen or sixteen, then come to dominate choice. Thirdly, the realistic period begins at seventeen with compromises based on reality taking place. Exploration leads to crystallisation, followed finally by specification in young adulthood.

By 1972, Ginzberg had modified his original theory, by making the following points. The process of choice is lifelong and open ended. He saw irreversibility as no longer valid, with individuals trying to keep their options open as long as possible. This may well be more possible in the United States, but the education system, in this country, is based on early specialization. Finally, rather than use "compromise", he suggests the term "optimisation" describes better what actually happens. Individuals seek to make the best of what they have to offer and of what is available.

Super (1981), while critical of Ginzberg et al's methodology, and describing the theory as speculative, does describe it as "rich in stimulating and likely looking ideas". It is certainly true that he has taken up the developmental theoretical position and spent the last three decades presenting and refining it, whilst Ginzberg has contributed little of substance to theorizing.

b.) Donald Super is probably the major figure in occupational choice theory. His work is extensive, spread over a long period of time, and based upon research on both sides of the Atlantic. His original ten propositions were amended to twelve (Super and Bactrach 1957), and are still valid in Super's estimation.

Proposition 1. People differ in their abilities, interests and personalities.

Proposition 2. They are qualified, by virtue of these characteristics, each for a number of occupations.

Proposition 3. Each of these occupations requires a characteristic pattern of abilities, interests, and personality traits, though with tolerances wide enough to allow both some variety of occupations for each individual and some variety of individuals in each occupation.

Proposition 4. Vocational preferences and competencies, the situations in which people live and work, and hence their self concepts, change with time and experience (although self concepts are generally fairly stable from late adolescence until late maturity), making choice and adjustment a continuous process.

Proposition 5. This process may be summed up in a series of life stages characterised as those of Growth, Exploration, Establishment, Maintenance, and Decline, and these stages may in turn be subdivided into

(a)the Fantasy, Tentative, and Realistic phases of the Exploratory stage, and

(b)the Trial and Stable phases of the Establishment stage.

Proposition 6. The nature of the career pattern (that is, the occupational level attained and the sequence, frequency and duration of trial and stable jobs) is determined by the individual's parental socio-economic level, mental ability, and personality characteristics, and by the opportunities to which he is exposed.

Proposition 7. Development through the life stages can be guided, partly by facilitating the process of maturation of abilities and interests, and partly by aiding in reality testing and in the development of self concept.

Proposition 8. The process of vocational development is essentially that of developing and implementing a self concept: it is a compromise process in which the self concept is a product of the interaction of inherited aptitudes, neural and endocrine make-up, opportunity to play various roles, and evaluations of the extent to which the results of role playing meet with the approval of superiors and fellows.

Proposition 9. The process of compromise between individual and social factors, between self concept and reality, is one of role playing, whether the role is played in fantasy , in the counselling interview, or in real-life activities such as school classes, clubs, part-time work, and entry jobs.

Proposition 10. Work satisfactions and life satisfactions depend upon the extent to which the individual finds adequate outlets for his abilties, interests, personality traits, and values; they depend upon his establishment in a type of work, a work situation, and a way of life in which he can play the kind of role which his growth and exploratory experiences have led him to consider congenial and appropriate.

Proposition 11. The degree of satisfaction the individual attains from his or her work is proportionate to the degree to which he or she has been able to implement self concepts.

Proposition 12. Work and occupation provide a focus for personality organisation for most men and women, although for some people this focus is peripheral, incidental, or even non-existent, and other foci such as social activities and the home are central.

Super's developmental approach is founded on five life stages, and these are described below.

1.) Growth (Birth to fourteen)

Fantasy (4-10) needs are dominant.
Interest (11-12)
Capacity (13-14) abilities are considered as well as job requirements.

2.) Exploration Stage (15-24)

Tentative (15-17) tentative choices are made and tried out in fantasy, discussions, and work.
Transition (18-21) reality factors are given more attention as the individual enters work, training or further education.
Trial (21-24) an apparently suitable choice is tried out.

3.) Establishment Stage (24-44)

Trial(24-30) Job or jobs are likely to be tested for suitablility.
Stabilization (31-44) A pattern emerges and the individual attempts to secure his position in work.

4.) Maintenance (44-64)

Work position is consolidated.

5.) Decline (65+)

Retirement or reduction in work role.

More recently, Super (1981) has used the concept of role to illustrate the variety of ways in which the individual conducts his life over a lifetime. In his life-career rainbow, there are nine potential roles which can be occupied at some stage. They are parent, homemaker, spouse, worker, citizen, leisurite, student, child and pensioner. These roles are conducted within four principal 'theatres' - home, community, education and work. This is a very helpful way of conceptualising the different areas of life experience and how they interact. It puts work into perspective by showing that it is one of many roles that we might adopt. Many people have been deprived of this role by unemployment, but this does not leave them without an identity or a role. It also illustrates how roles can conflict and create problems, e.g. work role and parent role.

Osipow (1973) regards Super's theory as a "well ordered, highly systematic representation of the processes of vocational motivation" although he felt that he had given insufficient attention to social and economic factors that influence career decisions. Since then, Super (1981) has produced a model that does give weight to 'situational determinents' i.e. social structure and economic conditions, as well as 'personal determinents', i.e. interests, values etc. However, Kline (1975) contends that Super's theory does not justify the name, because it does not give any new insights into vocational guidance.

Super's work, as we saw in chapter one, has stimulated the practice of careers programmes in British schools. By stressing the developmental nature of occupational choice and the possibility of positive interventions in this process, Super has laid a theoretical basis for careers education. This has been supported early on by Daws(1968) and subsequently by other sources such as the Schools Council, N.I.C.E.C. and the Inspectorate, in various publications.

4. Social Learning Theory.

In the late seventies, social learning theory was applied to occupational choice by a group of American researchers. Their work was published by Mitchell, Jones and Krumboltz (1979) and they state that it

> "attempts to encompass a total process, not just some phase of it. It explains the development of career aspirations and achievements which are so important in the trait-factor approach; reinforces the notion that career selection is a developmental process at the same time (although contesting the validity of lock-stop developmental stages and phases); clarifies the role of decision making and evolution of decision making

skills; allows for the influence of economic and sociological variables; and is compatible with critical aspects of personality theories".

This approach grew out of the work of Banduba in the 1960's, which emphasised modelling in behaviour acquisition. Thus, people learn not just from the consequences of their own responses but also from the observation of other people's behaviour and its consequences for them. Mitchell et al state that four factors influence career decision making.

1.) Genetic endowment, i.e. race, sex, intelligence and special abilities.

2.) Environmental conditions and events, e.g. family experience and training opportunities.

3.) Learning experiences, e.g. instrumental and associative learning.

4.) Task approach skills, e.g. learning skills.

Three types of consequences arise from these four influences:

1.) Self-observation generalisations, e.g. "I'm good at English".

2.) Task approach skills, e.g. seeking information about work.

3.) Actions, e.g. applying for a course of study.

Genetic endowment and environmental conditions are clearly beyond the control of the client or counsellor, but this is not the case with learning experiences and task approach skills. Instrumental learning experiences are those where the individual acts on the environment so as to produce certain outcomes. On the other hand, associative learning experiences occur when the individual pairs two events so that he or she associates a previously neutral situation with some positive or negative reaction. Task approach skills cover a wide range, for instance, thought processes and performance standards. Clearly, there are many ways of improving these skills through individual or group means.

Self observation generalisations result from learning experiences and, of course, are not always accurate. Values are a type of self observation generalisation. Using interests and profiling them, by means of questionnaires, is a usual and valid way of establishing a pattern of these generalisations.

Krumboltz (1976) draws a number of implications of his theory for counsellors.

> 1.)"Occupational placement is the result of a complex interaction of genetic components, environmental events and conditions and learning experiences which result in the development of various task approach skills". This emphasises the mixture of 'nature' and 'nurture' involved in the process of occupational placement.
>
> 2.)"Career selection is a mutual process influenced not only by decisions made by each individual involved, but also by social forces which effect occupational availability and requirements. People select, and are selected by, occupations". The statement emphasises the supply and demand elements in occupational entity, which impose a 'reality'on ultimate occupational choice.
>
> 3.)"Career selection is a lifelong process. It does not take place at one point in time, but is shaped by events and decisions that occur from infancy, through to the retirement years". As with Super, the development aspects are stressed from the early years to later adulthood.
>
> 4.)"Career selection is caused, not accidental, but the interaction of causal events is so complex that the prediction of occupational selection for any one individual is virtually impossible with any degree of certainty". If Krumboltz is correct, this makes 'traditional' vocational guidance, which was largely based on prediction and forecast, an invalid exercise.

5.)"Career indecision is due to the unsatisfactory nature or an insufficient number of career relevant learning experiences or to the fact that the person has not yet learned and applied a systematic way of making career decisions. Indecision is a natural result of not having had certain learning experiences. An undecided person has no reason to feel guilty or inadequate". The ability to make career decisions is directly related to relevant learning experiences. The implication from this is clear; that the school or counsellor can help provide some of these experiences through offering work experience, for example, which can then enable the client to make some of the necessary decisions more effectively.

6.)"Career counselling is not merely a process of matching personal characteristics with existing job characteristics, but instead, is a process of opening up new learning experiences and motivating a client to initiate career-relevant exploratory activities". This statement expands the role of vocational guidance from diagnostic and assessment to a broader developmental role, which suggests that the counsellor produces a programme of activities designed to help his clients learn (rather than be told).

7.)"The responsiblities of a career counsellor, then, are as follows:

a.)to help the client learn a rational sequence of career decision making skills.

b.)To help the client arrange an appropriate sequence of career-relevant exploratory learning experiences, and

c.)To teach the client how to evaluate the personal consequences of these learning experiences.

Finally, this statement makes a clear case for a carers education programme which would provide pupils with a variety of learning experiences, give them the opportunity to evaluate these experiences, so as to maximise learning, and then to encourage them to develop their decision-making skills in order to utilise what they have learnt.

5.) Decision-Making.

Assuming that an individual has some choice of occupation, however, minimal, the question of decision making must arise. In recent years, the more general matter of decision making has aroused interest in education and there have been moves to teach decision making skills as an 'essential life skill'. There are a number of theories of vocational decision making and they will be discussed briefly.

Some decision making theories are broadly speaking 'descriptive'. Tiedeman and O'Hara (1963) produced such a model that looks at decision making as a two part process; anticipation and implementation - adjustment. Anticipation begins with exploration which involves the individual visualising himself in working situations. Crystallization follows this with an attempt to assess personal values in relation to possible occupations whilst also weighing the relative advantages and disadvantages. Stabilization is beginning to occur and this leads to a choice, which then stimulates action.

Gelatt (1962) produced a prescriptive model that can be used in vocational counselling. A need to decide is precipitated by a purpose, i.e. to chose an occupation. This leads to a need for information, i.e. what jobs are available, what could I do, etc. Gelatt suggests that this information is organised into three systems:

1.)prediction - possible alternative actions, possible outcomes, probable outcomes,

2.)relative preferences based on value system,

3.)evaluation and selection of criteria.

As an example - a boy might see a number of jobs in the building trade as alternatives, from his knowledge, perhaps based on father and friends. Plumbing and bricklaying are possibilities, with bricklaying most likely, because of greater availability of work. In terms of desirability, bricklaying seems best, as there is more money to be earned, but he isn't too sure about the regularity of work in this type of job. Therefore, he has to evaluate what information he has, in order to arrive at a decision. In doing this, he finds that he doesn't know too much about plumbing, thus he seeks more information about the work from his careers teacher, and a friend, who knows someone who is plumber.

This information is 'fed back' into the three systems, but is now added to another idea, gas fitting, suggested by his careers teacher. All three jobs are subjected to prediction, relative preferences, and evaluation before coming to an actual decision, brought about by a closing date for applications for gas fitting training. The process, outlined above, does constitute a workable model representing the process that occurs in making decisions. By formalising it, individuals can be helped to systematise these processes and produce a decision that has more clearly been thought out.

6.) Autonomy.

Law (1981) has suggested a third way of understanding the process of occupational choice. This chapter has outlined the two well established theoretical perspectives of differentialism and developmentalism. Law sees both the degree of autonomy assigned to the individual and the terms in which the statements of autonomy are made as enlightening. Autonomy has a variety of meanings, but can be seen to include self direction, control of one's actions as well as personal freedom and responsibility.

The extent to which it is valid to think of people as being autonomous has been the subject of much debate by social scientists. Law describes this debate, and in doing so, points to autonomy as being thought of as a variable feature of personality, dependent on the nature of society at any moment of time, or, alternatvely, the result of different organismic capacities. Likewise, it can be seen as a progressively acquired characteristic in individual development; something that some individuals acquire as part of their maturational process. In recent years, autonomy has been conceived of as a goal for programmes of personal and careers education.

Law conceptualises autonomy on a scale where, at one extreme the individual can be seen as having no autonomy, whilst at the other, there is personal striving and the achievement of chosen goals. Roberts (1977) ascribes little or no autonomy to the individual as regards his occupational choice, and goes so far as to suggest that 'choice' is an inappropriate word to use. Work is therefore something that individuals enter, rather than choose, being determined by the availability of jobs, and by the education system, through which they pass.

The notion of self consciousness, self awareness and of implementing a self concept through work are all bound up with autonomy and occupational choice. Self assertion and self determination are other terms which extend the boundaries of autonomy. Choice, as a term, implies multiple awareness of both opportunities and of personal potential. Personal striving relies heavily on a conception of the future and a combination of both self belief, and a trust in the nature of society to respond to individual initiatives. In philosophical terms, this view of man is embodied in existentialism, which conceives of man as being endowed with will and consciousness. Man, aware of his mortality, seeks his own destiny and identity by means of his own actions.

In discussing autonomy, it is appropriate to refer to the work of George Kelly, who has become a leading figure in psychology. Kelly's work on a theory of personal constructs (1955) has heralded a new approach to both psychological theory and practice, and both are of relevance to vocational guidance. Kelly rejected the proposition that individuals are directed by their genes or by their environment, solely. He stated that, in order to understand man, it is necessary to consider each individual's construction of reality. Man is a 'scientist, actively trying to make sense of his world', according to Kelly. To do this , he has to try and impose some structure on his experiences by looking for recurring themes or patterns, which Kelly describes as 'constructs'.

Kelly set out his theory as a series of postulates which are briefly summarised as follows. Man anticipates the future and checks out how well his experience of the past has enabled him to do this. Themes recur, but do not remain exactly the same, because man is "in motion". Man's personal constructs are based on what he has learnt, they embody his values, and are a statement of his intent. Constructs are best seen as having two poles; positive and negative. People are similar, because they construe in the same way.

Bannister and Fransella (1977) have been prominent in promoting Kelly's work, in the U.K. They are critical of much of psychology for separating personality theory off from the rest of the discipline, and for studying individual differences by seeking group sameness. They quote Kelly on the subject of roles. Roles have seen Man, either in terms of his economic priorities, or conforming more broadly to ideologies. Kelly suggests that society is composed of 'inquiring' persons.

When Kelly came to assessing people, he introduced the idea of a repertory grid. This is a means of eliciting the relationships for a person between sets of constructs. The aim is to reveal the patterning of constructs for a person rather than relating this to some set of norms. It has no fixed form of content, like a test, but statistical tests of significance can be applied to the set of comparisons that each person has made. The repertory grid will be examined in more detail, as a practical tool in vocational guidance, in Chapter 7.

Kelly made much of the fact that psychologists were suspicious of direct personal statements, and consequently made their tests oblique, often including scales to identify any lies made whilst completing the tests. He believed that inviting the individual to say something about himself, self-characterisation, was a more useful means of learning about people. Clients are invited to write this self-characterisation in the third person to reduce any threat. This sort of account can give all sorts of clues about the individual, and how well he relates and understands others. As Bannister and Fransella put it "our signal failure to measure the person derives from our habit of asking him to answer our questions rather than noting the nature of the questions which he is asking".

Summary

Theories serve a number of purposes and therefore can be assessed by a variety of criteria.

Broadly speaking, they seek to provide explanations of complex phenomena, and in doing so, sometimes produce the means to influence and change human behaviour. Vocational guidance is essentially a practical activity, but is dealing with some very complex issues, and thus needs to be underpinned by some theoretical base. As we have seen, psychology has provided a number of theories and explanations of occupational choice. Some of these theories have features in common, whilst others are quite different.

A comparison of theories should help to show their relative value to those working in vocational guidance. Osipow(1973) suggests a number of criteria which can be usefully applied to compare theories of occupational choice. These are; their explanatory adequacy, how far they are supported empirically, the simplicity of their concepts, how useful they are to both research and practice, and how consistent they are. He maintains that the theories are descriptive rather than explanatory. Thus for example, the trait and factor approach merely describes individuals and occupations in certain terms without explaining why this should be so. Roe and the psycho-analytic writers focus on needs to attempt some explanation but this then raises the next question of empirical support.

There are serious deficiencies here, according to Osipow, partly because of the difficulties of investigating concepts such as psychic energy, which Roe uses. Two fundamental aspects of Super's theory; self concept implementation and its importance, and the serious of career development tasks which must be made in a lifetime have been confirmed by research evidence. The samples used by some researchers have been criticised, e.g. Ginzberg, too narrow in class in class and ethnic terms; Holland, excluded women. The question of how widely these theories can be applied between different cultures is important. Roberts(1968) maintained that Ginzberg's and Super's theories were inapplicable in Britain because of crucial cultural differences, between this country and the States.

The theories in this chapter do assume a universal application, and psychological theories are open to criticism for their lack of attention to the social and cultural context in which individuals live, and the differences that exist between these contexts. It is interesting to see

Super drawing more heavily upon sociological concepts such as 'role' in his later work. Certainly, when examining the strengths and limitations of any one discipline's theories, it does underline the need for an interdisciplinary approach to the subject of occupational choice.

Osipow(1973) sees all the theories as not over complex in their use of concepts. When it comes to the application of these theories, in research or in practice, Super and Holland have exercised most influence in both spheres in recent years. The early impact of trait and factor theory has been emphasised. However, in the last twenty years, Super's work has become more influential, whilst Holland has made a considerable impact in the States. Both have produced instruments for use in vocational guidance, which have had varying degrees of acceptance.

As Osipow points out, some of the theories are attempting to do different things and are thus not easy to compare. In conclusion, he says that

> "as a conceptual model, Super's theory seems to be most highly developed and advanced. This is reflected in its explicitness, its fairly high degree of empirical support and its substantially larger number of applications to human affairs. The personality style approach, on the other hand, seems to be the most amenable to the experimental and scientific method, and the closest to basic psychological concepts, but still lacking in a wide base of empirical support".

Chapter Three

SOCIOLOGICAL EXPLANATIONS OF OCCUPATIONAL CHOICE

"Any lack of deference to careers work is not because sociologists prefer to be useless. Quite the reverse; eventually a sociological perspective can encourage practitioners to pose more penetrating questions".
(K. Roberts. 'Career Development in Britain', 1981.)

Sociology, by definition, is concerned more with group processes, than with the individual. It seeks to understand the way in which society is structured, how these structures change over time, and the impact that these structures have upon individuals and their 'life chances'. By structures, we mean the family, education, religion, work, the media, and the State. For instance sociologists are interested in the transition from school to work and how this is determined. However, it is true to say that it is only in recent years that sociology has addressed itself to the sorts of questions that those working in vocational guidance are interested in. Consequently there is not the same body of writing and research in this field, in comparison with the output of psychologists. This probably reflects the notion that occupational choice is primarily an individual process, although this chapter will seek to question this view.

As with the other social sciences, Sociology has been concerned with developing theories in order to explain social phenomena. It is obviously important to examine a number of the more important theories to see how they explain occupational choice as a social, rather than as an individual process. Functionalism is one of the oldest schools of sociological thought, and although it has been vigorously challenged by other schools of thought, still warrants attention. It has been defined as the analysis of social and cultural phenomena in terms of the functions they perform in a sociocultural system. In functionalism, society is conceived of as a system of interrelated parts, in which no part can be understood in isolation from the whole. A change in any part is seen as leading to a certain degree of imbalance, which in turn results in changes in other parts of the system, and to some extent to a re-organisation of the system as a whole. The development of functionalism was based on the model of the organic system in the biological sciences. Hence the emphasis of functionalism is upon the integration of society, with the proposition that change in one part of the system is accommodated by change in another part of the system in order to restore equilibrium.

If we apply this theoretical perspective to the transition from education to work, both occupational choice and occupational entry would need to be examined. It is important to emphasise these as two separate entities as they do not necessarily correspond for all individuals. This distinction is one that is made more readily by sociologists that psychologists. Functionalism sees individuals being prepared or socialised for work by both their family, and the education system. The family provides role models for each individual, with father in his main role as a paid worker and mother, in her main role as an unpaid worker. Individuals are encouraged to achieve within the education system, by both family and school, so that they can enter appropriate work roles when it is time for them to leave.

The implications of this functionalist interpretation of occupational entry are several. The process is seen as basically smooth with family and school linked together by similar objectives, with the individual complying with the requirements of both. The education system is likewise linked to employment in the sense that it recognises its role of preparing its students for work. This is reflected in the curriculum, which changes in response to the altering demands of the economy. For example, the growth of a computer industry has meant that computing is now taught in all areas of education. In other words, this is a functional response of one institution to another.

In fact, this sort of response is enshrined in the technical function theory of education. This proposes that the skill requirements of jobs in industrial societies increase steadily because of technological change. Two processes occur. Jobs requiring low skill decrease in number, with an increase in the number of jobs requiring high skill, whilst the same jobs are upgraded in skill requirements. In turn, education provides the training necessary for the more highly skilled jobs. The result is that educational requirements for jobs constantly rise, and increasing numbers of the population are required to spend longer periods within education. This theory is part of the wider functionalist perspective , that, for example, sees social stratification resulting from occupations requiring particular skills, and these skills being supplied by those people who have the natural ability, and the necessary education and training; a 'meritocracy' in a sense.

The Careers Service, and those involved in vocational guidance, would be seen as having an important role, in functionalist terms. They can link together family, education and work, by providing information, advice and help to all those institutions, as well as to the individual. This role could be seen as increasingly important in advanced industrial societies, whose technological change is particularly rapid. Vocational guidance practitioners have an important function in keeping up to date with changes in the patterns of employment, so that students can be accurately informed and advised, thus ensuring that they are helped to find suitable jobs, and that employers get the most suitable employees. In this way, the economy is served, and individuals find an appropriate occupational role. It is probably fair to say that many of those people engaged in vocational guidance would broadly subscribe to the functionalist perspective, without describing it as such.

However, for some time now, functionalism has been challenged as being an inadequate theoretical perspective. It has problems in explaining both conflict, within society, and the lack of linkage between various institutions. Likewise, it can be seen as a theoretical explanation that sees society essentially in terms of consensus, with conflict explained as deviant. As an example, the current high level of unemployment would be difficult to explain in functionalist terms. Both Secondary and Higher Education are 'producing' large numbers of well qualified students, many of whom fail to get a job appropriate to their education, or any job at all. Careers officers have a changed and limited role in this situation. Perhaps the Youth Training Scheme can be seen as a state inspired response to change (and potential conflict), which might be regarded as functional. However, it is unlikely to be effective unless there are sufficient jobs for YTS trainees to enter after training.

Some sociological theories do emphasise the nature of conflict within society, and these offer a different explanation of occupational entry. Max Weber, the German sociologist, saw society composed of groups competing for wealth, power or prestige. He identified status groups as one of the basic units of society; these groups being comprised of persons who share a sense of status equally based on participation in a common culture, i.e. style of language, taste, manners, opinions, values. The individual's sense of identity springs from his status group membership. Status groups do not have distinct boundaries, and are fluid and overlapping. They derive from differences in the 'market' situation, based on economic factors, differences in life situation, based upon power, and differences in life style deriving from various factors such as education, religion and ethnicity. A good deal of power, wealth and prestige is to be gained from work, and thus members of status groups compete for entry to occupations. This struggle tends to be between status groups, rather than within them.

Status groups use education as a means of maintaining status culture. Collins (1972) argues that education is less concerned with the acquisition of skills than with imparting status culture. Education provides training for the elite culture, or respect for it, and employers use education as a means of selection for cultural attributes. Putting this in the context of British schools, the leading Public Schools are seen as educating an elite. Grammar Schools modelled themselves upon these schools, whilst Secondary Modern Schools tried to inculcate a respect for academic education (and often reinforced the second rate status of non-academic subjects). Comprehensive Schools have blurred some of these distinctions, but it could be argued that the hierarchies still exist, and serve to inhibit social mobility.

Social Class

There is a considerable amount of empirical evidence to support this explanation, although the relationship between social class, education and education is a complex one. This is made more complex by rapid change in the structure of occupations, and within education. The most recent major study of social mobility was led by Halsey (1980), and used the life histories of a national sample of 10,000 men in 1972. The study showed a growing middle class of professional, managerial and administrative occupations,and both a declining lower middle class of supervisors, technicians, small shopkeepers etc., plus a working class of manual workers. Class of origin, based on father's occupation was compared with class of desination, based on the individual's occupation ten years after entry to work. This comparison showed 55.4% remaining within the same class with 44.6% moving either upwards or downwards in class terms; quite a degree of social mobility. When the relative chances of moving from given origns to given destinations is examined however, the chances of becoming middle class are highest for middle class sons, with more than half retaining their position, while fewer than one in nine working class sons have moved into the middle class.

Social mobility and certain educational criteria seem to provide an answer as Table 3.1 shows. Halsey commenting on this table says "it is equally clear that moblity involves realignment of social class membership according to qualifications. Thus, those who have moved upwards have, in the process, exceeded the educational norms of their origin group, and those who have moved downwards have had less educational advantage and attained fewer education qualfications. This pattern is absolutely regular". He also questions the apparently high levels of social mobility by pointing out that expanding middle class occupational opportunities have been shared out fairly equally to men of different class origins with the result that "relative class chances have been stable or increasingly unequal".

The Oxford study is now ten years old, but Halsey maintains that the last decade has seen no significant change in "social distribution of educational achievement" despite comprehensive reorganisation and the abolition of Direct Grant schools. This is linked to his assertion that education is "essentially not to create but to re-create society, not to form structures of social life but to maintain the people and the skills

Table 3.1 Education & Mobility

	Private Primary Schooling %	Selective Secondary Schooling %	School Exams. %	Some F.E. Qualifications %	Univ. Degree %
1. Stable middle-class	32.0	88.4	82.0	33.1	29.8
2. Middle to lower-middle	24.9	65.1	53.6	17.2	5.7
3. Middle to working	3.8	33.5	15.1	7.0	0.5
4. Lower-middle to middle	11.7	67.9	62.1	34.1	13.5
5. Stable lower-middle	7.5	44.3	27.1	5.6	1.0
6. Lower-middle to working	3.0	21.9	8.1	1.8	0.1
7. Working to middle	1.6	63.1	58.5	32.3	12.8
8. Working to lower-middle	2.0	32.2	20.2	3.9	1.1
9. Stable working	0.6	14.7	4.6	0.4	0.1
ALL	5.8	34.8	23.9	10.3	4.3

that inform these structures". In other words, education at all levels is essentially a conservative institution, responding to other institutions, rather than initiating any substantial change within society. As part of the educational system, the Careers Service can be seen similarly.

This basically 'passive' role of education accords with Bowles and Gintis (1976) 'correspondence principle'. This purports that the experience of education directly anticipates the experience of work and the economic system. Pupils are instilled with

> "the idea of differential rewards for success and failure, grouping and promotion based on performance, hierarchy and authority, and externally imposed tasks and timetables. Further progress in the educational ladder is reflected in changes in the conditions and status of the pupils as they gradually come to be identified as a future elite. Those who drop out have already clearly been identified as failures, deserving of lower status and reward".

This explanation of the relationship between the education system and work is shared by Willis (1977) in his study of working class youth. In explaining how working class boys end up in working class jobs, he says

> "It is the school which has built up a certain resistance to mental work and an inclination towards manual work. At least manual work is outside the domain of school and carries with it - though not intrinsically - the aura of the real adult world. Resistance to mental work becomes resistance to authority as learnt at school ..... Thus physical labouring comes to stand for and express, most importantly, a kind of masculinity and also an opposition to authority - at least as it is learned in school".

Social class dimensions can be seen to influence occupational entry at all levels of education. In 1960, a major study of undergraduates was conducted by Kelsall (1972). The findings led to the following comment

> "For the University graduates in this study clearly did not have equal opportunities in the world of work, even if they experienced an identical form of education and had performed equally well or badly. They were (aside from their qualifications) not part of a common culture, but had come to University with attitudes profoundly influenced by their family backgrounds and there were, in many cases, reinforced and certainly not attenuated by the process of Higher Education itself. When they came to seek employment in the particularly high status sections, social class influences were reinforced by the images and preferences of the prospective employers themselves".

Some ten years later, Gothard (1982) carried out a similar study, and his findings confirmed Kelsall's study. Students from middle class homes and from public schools were highly overrepresented at University and at Oxbridge in particular. Oxbridge students continued to enter higher status occupations in greater proportions than students at other universities, and were also less likely to be unemployed. This study also confirmed the findings of a number of earlier studies (Marris,1964, Abbott,1971, Jackson and Marsden,1962) when it showed that university students from working class homes often had considerable problems of adjustment and identity, which related directly to their entry to a particularly middleclass institution, the University.

The National Child Development Study (NCDS) is the largest longitudinal study to be conducted in recent years. In 1974, its sample of 10,869 was 16 years old and the study examined the educational and occupational aspirations of the sample (Fogelman, 1979). Table 3.2 shows the differences in occupational aspirations amongst both boys and girls from different social classes.

The differences between boys and girls is just as notable as those between social classes. This gender difference will be explored later in this chapter.

Table 3.2 Aspired job - by sex and social class

	Social Class									
	I & II		III NM		III M		IV & V		No male head	
	B %	G %	B %	G %	B %	G %	B %	G %	B %	G %
Outdoor	5	3	3	4	3	2	5	2	4	2
Artistics etc.	5	8	8	4	4	4	4	4	5	5
Teachers	4	18	3	8	2	9	1	7	2	8
Professions	29	10	16	4	10	2	7	1	8	2
Other Professions	11	7	10	8	9	4	8	3	5	3
Caring	1	15	0.4	18	0.4	19	0.1	18	1	20
Shopworkers	2	5	2	11	2	13	2	15	2	13
Other Services	4	5	5	6	7	5	6	4	7	4
Clerical	4	20	4	28	3	32	3	30	2	30
Building	3	0	5	0	9	0	11	0.2	11	0
Engineering	12	0.2	21	1	28	0.4	27	0.4	26	0
Other Industrial	4	1	5	1	9	4	11	9	8	6
Forces and MN	6	1	10	1	9	2	10	4	13	3
Uncertain	10	8	8	6	6	5	6	4	7	5
N (=100%)	1093	1020	507	438	1890	1829	815	771	322	343

Table 3.3 Educational plans - by sex and social class

	Social Class									
	I & II		III NM		III M		IV & V		No male head	
	B %	G %	B %	G %	B %	G %	B %	G %	B %	G %
University or polytechnic	31	22	16	10	7	6	6	3	7	5
College of education	3	11	3	9	2	8	2	5	2	6
Other full-time from 17/18	4	11	3	5	2	4	2	3	2	6
Part-time from 17/18	10	9	8	6	6	6	5	5	8	5
No study from 17/18	3	2	2	3	2	2	1	1	2	1
Uncertain from 17/18	6	5	3	4	2	3	2	1	3	2
Full-time from 16	5	12	4	9	4	8	4	5	2	8
Part-time from 16	19	12	34	23	40	24	38	25	38	27
No study from 16	8	8	10	16	16	21	22	26	18	21
Uncertain from 16	4	3	8	9	11	15	14	19	11	11
Other	9	6	11	7	7	5	5	6	8	8
N (=100%)	1148	1143	523	454	1976	1885	840	793	336	353

Table 3.3 again looks at the social class of the boys and girls but considers their educational plans. Again it is both differences between social class groups and between boys and girls that is interesting.

GENDER

Social class divisions have preoccupied sociologists for many decades. Gender and ethnic divisions have become the focus of attention rather more recently, although there is a lot of evidence to suggest that they are both highly significant in determining occupational entry. There has been an 'explosion' of books and articles on the subject of sexual divisions in society and it is only possible to refer to some of the literature in this field. Differences in employment patterns between men and women clearly indicate that there is a sexual division of labour, and the reasons for this will be explored as this has a direct bearing on both theories of occupational choice and vocational guidance.

In 1981, women accounted for about 41% of the total workforce. 64% of women between 16 - 60 work, 25% of them part-time. Two thirds of women at work were married. One in ten families, with children under 16, had a woman as sole breadwinner. The proportion of women working, and the extent of part-time work varies with age; but of those women aged 35-49, 69% were working whilst 97% of men aged 35-49 were working. It has been estimated that, on average, women are likely to be out of paid employment for a total of seven years while they are forming a family. In 1980, 30% of women with a child under 4 years old were working, whilst a total of 54% of women with dependent children were working. These figures illustrate the degree of involvement of women of all ages, in the labour force, in Britain today. However, women have always been a substantial percentage of the total labour force, although a 'myth' has existed that they constitute a small unimportant element, in comparison with men.

Ruth Miller (1981) makes the point that "despite the increase in numbers of women at work, there has been no corresponding increase in the spread of jobs they do, or the industries they work in. Over half of all women in manual work are still concentrated in a narrow range of low paid skill industries and occupations - mainly in textiles, catering, hairdressing, laundries, cleaning and light engineering assembly work". If non-manual occupational groups are considered, women are heavily concentrated in clerical work (33.6%), professional and related in health, welfare education (15.3%) and selling(8.1%), whilst men are much more evenly distributed within occupational groups. When highly paid, professional occupations are considered, the following pattern emerges

<u>Percentage of Women (1980)</u>

Bank Managers	1
Directors of 100 top UK companies	<1
Full members of Institute of Chartered Accountants	4
Full members of Institute of Civil Engineers	0.25
Full members of Institute of Electrical Engineers	0.16
Full members of Royal Institute of Chartered Surveyors	0.9
Practising Dentists	17
Practising G.P.s	17
Practising Surgeons	0.8
Practising Barristers	10
Practising Solicitors	8
Practising Architects	5
Practising Veterinary Surgeons	10
University Professors	2
Local Authority Chief Executives	<1

In order to understand the reasons for this striking difference in range and level of employment, it is necessary to examine ways in which girls learn to be women (and boys learn to be men). The family is the earliest source of gender models and it is where boys and girls learn their respective roles. Although, as we have seen that women, including those with dependent children, are active in the labour force, there is a general expectation that their primary role, is or will be within the home, as wife and mother. A married woman's role, in paid employment, is seen as of secondary importance, with her commitment seen as less and her motivation as lower than that of a man. She works for 'pin money'. This view of the 'working' woman is often given as the reason for womens' position in the occupational structure, and although it has always been challenged, and more so today, it remains the "conventional wisdom".

It is within this context that girls and boys learn their future roles. A recent study examined a group of first year pupils at an urban comprehensive school, by asking their parents about their educational and occupational aspirations for them (Kelly et al, 1982). The study also examined the parents' views on sexual equality and their childrens' out of school activities. The parents had high educational aspirations for their children, particularly for their daughters, and didn't differentiate to any extent between the sexes as regards the relative importance of subjects studied.

However, differences did emerge when occupational aspirations were considered. Jobs were sex-stereotyped, on traditional lines, to a large extent, with doctor, manager and computer operator as exceptions. It was also noticeable that the parents felt that it was important that boys got jobs that were secure, with good prospects, whilst girls were seen to require interesting work of their own preference. The parents were asked a number of questions to estimate their level of sexist thinking. From this it emerged that working class fathers expressed the most sexist views whilst middle class 'working' mothers who had only daughters, expressed the least sexist views. It was interesting to note differences in household tasks performed by the children. Girls spent a good deal more of their time on these tasks, and the tasks were largely sex-stereotyped i.e. girls doing cooking, boys washing the car. This pattern was also born out by the parent's household tasks. Although 64% of the women were in paid employment, only a small proportion of the men helped regularly with the household tasks.

The conclusions drawn from this study are interesting, as they could be seen to reflect the way in which parents think and act more generally within Britain today. A formal commitment to equality coexisted with other attitudes, which tended to make true equality impossible. Quoting Kelly et al

> "Children are mainly the woman's responsibility and they are her main

> responsibility. Women have the right to work, but only if they can do so, without detriment to their maternal and domestic roles. These parents do not see equality of the sexes as necessitating any great change in the way society is organised. Equality is a little something extra, which can be added on to existing social arrangements........ Most parents would not oppose their child getting a job stereotypically associated with the opposite sex. However, they do not envisage this happening".

Ann Oakley (1981) reviews early socialisation and draws on a number of studies. She describes a situation in which girls and boys are treated differently from birth. Sharpe (1976) talks of the early unconscious process of differentiation, being later overlaid with more explicit practices. This takes a variety of forms. Mothers make more fuss over the appearance of their daughters, reinforcing society's views on the importance of feminine beauty. Toys are sexually stereotyped, and childrens' books confirm these stereotypes. Parents use different language to praise or criticise boys and girls. Archer and Lloyd (1982) provide a useful summary of this process.

> "The individual comes into the world with no set notion of what male and female are, but develops this classification process at about two years of age; subsequently this is elaborated and used as a way of making sense of the social world and of guiding action...... Eventually he or she comes to regard their own culturally induced variety of gender differences as equivalent to the natural order of things".

Differences between boys and girls continue to manifest themselves within the education system, with boys attaining relatively superior achievements. The Tables on the next pages illustrate this.

Table 3.4 Entries at 'O' Level & 'A' Level (thousands) 1979

'O' Level	Male	Female	'A' Level	Male	Female
English Lang	229	268	English	19	41
Maths	171	137	Maths	41	13
Biology	83	140	Biology	18	21
Physics	123	39	Physics	40	9
Chemistry	84	50	Chemistry	29	13
Cookery	1.6	52	Art	9	13
T.D.	54	1.9	French	9	17
Total (all subjects)	1470	1480	Total	312	243

(Source D.E.S.)

Table 3.5 Undergraduate entrants to University & Polytechnic 1979/80

	University		Poly	
	Male	Female	Male	Female
Medicine	2755	1788	-	-
Dentistry	702	397	-	-
Engineering	11395	819	3663	39
Biol.Sciences	938	771	344	148
Mathematics	2900	1206	426	110
Physics	2218	379	115	5
Accounting	590	170	345	64
Psychology	429	851	95	92
French	208	910	187	327
Total (all students)	49457	31499	14470	8281

(Source U.C.C.A.)

Table 3.6 Further & Higher Education
(% of school leavers entering full-time further and higher education)

	Men	Women
Degree Course	8.6	6.3
Teacher Training	0.1	0.6
HND/HNC/OND/ONC	0.8	0.5
Catering	0.5	1.5
Nursing	-	1.7
Secretarial	-	5.0
GCE 'A'	2.0	2.7
GCE 'O'	1.4	1.7
Other & not known	4.3	7.1
All	17.7	27.1

(Source D.E.S.)

There are a number of explanations for these differences. The biological explanation has a long history, and Archer and Lloyd (1982) point to psychological testing as a fairly recent attempt to 'scientifically' measure and to establish any differences between groups such as men and women. They state that "the examination of careful tests of intellectual functioning is one of limited differences between men and women. Stereotypes cannot be readily reinforced by this evidence." King (1974) makes the important point that concerning differences between the sexes as regards physique, ability, personality, interests and values, "there is more basic similarity between them on all aspects of functioning". He also points out the sex roles assigned to each sex are likely to affect attitudes to testing itself, with boys responding in an achieving manner, and girls in a more submissive way.

The sex differentiation that is apparent in some areas of the curriculum has one of its sources in unequal provision. An HMI Report (1980) showed that 65% of the schools in its sample considered woodwork and metalwork more appropriate for boys, and home economics and needlework more appropriate for girls. Girls were not deliberately excluded from the physical sciences, but in some schools teachers expressed the view that boys should study physics, and girls, biology. For example, sometimes physics was set against home economics or typing, on the timetable. One reason suggested for girls relative lack of success in subjects such as mathematics lies in the group dynamics of the Classroom (Spender 1980). There is evidence that boys demand more attention in class and that teachers respond, by giving them more attention. In this situation, girls become less involved in lessons, and are dismissed more easily, with the result that they lose confidence, and become negative in their attitudes to subjects which tend to be regarded as essentially male.

The comparative performance of girls in mixed and single sex schools has been an issue of debate, (Dale 1975, Spender 1982). The most recent study (Steedman 1983) shows that girls in single sex schools achieve greater examination success, but this is because they tend to be brighter to start with, not because of the effect of single sex education. (Many all-girls schools are selective). Although girls in single sex schools do show more willingness to study science and technology, they are not more likely to study them because some girls' schools do not offer them.

Sharpe(1976) maintains that "girls are still schooled with the marriage market in mind, although this may not be acknowledged consciously". For instance, Parentcraft is a subject exclusively for girls, despite the fact that most boys will be parents at some stage of their life! Browne (1981) suggests that a process operates whereby certain types of knowledge and skills are projected as more appropriate for one sex, than another. Through the learning process, pupils learn not only 'subjects' but develop self concepts, and these self concepts may be based more on stereotypical than individual characteristics. They limit the type of skills and knowledge which pupils can develop, which in turn limits .the type of occupations open to them. This is especially true of girls and their tendency not to study physics and chemistry. By studying home based subjects, girls are reinforcing the view that their main responsiblity lies in family and domestic duties.

Higher Education could be seen as offering women the opportunity to 'break out' of these stereotypes. However, Table 3.5 shows women studying the less vocational subjects. Havinghurst has suggested a model (Figure 1) that helps to explain this phenomenon, as well as offering an explanation for the low proportion of working class students at University.

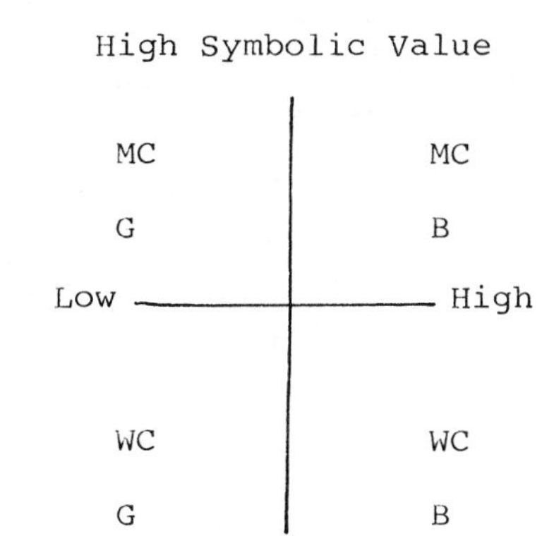

The two axes represent the levels of symbolic and functional value attached to education. Symbolic value has a status confirming function, whilst functional value relates to the relationship between certification and occupations. At one extreme, middle class boys attach both high functional and symbolic value to education, whilst at the other extreme, working class girls attach both low symbolic and functional value to education. This is illustrated by the figures for both groups that emerged from two major surveys of the undergraduate population (Kelsall, 1972, Gothard, 1982). In 1960, 43.4% of undergraduates were middle class boys; in 1976, the figure was 44%. In 1960, 5.3% of undergraduates were working class girls; in 1976, the figure was 5%.

Kelsall (1972) noted that "the vast majority (of graduate women) undoubtedly perceive their lives to be dominated by having children and looking after a home". This comment was repeated by Cherry (1975), based upon another large sample of students. By 1976-7, when Gothard (1982) was carrying out his study, there appeared to be a notable shift in attitude by women undergraduates. A much larger group were committed to the idea of a career, rather than committing themselves to marriage and a family. This was borne out by 75% perceiving themselves as ambitious, or more ambitious than their male contemporaries. When asked about the possibility of being discriminated against in employment interviews, half said that they expected this to happen, whilst one eighth didn't know. This was despite the fact that the Sex Discrimination Act had been passed a year before.

Reference has already been made to the limited range and low level of work entered by women. This is reinforced by the fact that womens' earnings are still only 73.5% of mens' earnings (D.E. Gazette, 1980). A number of studies confirm the fact that girls also aspire to a limited range of occupations (Rauta and Hunt,1975, Sharpe,1976, Fogelman, 1976, West and Newton,1983). These choices are predominantly clerical work; teaching, nursing and shop work. This continues to some extent with women graduates, who are more likely to enter teaching, nursing, social work, retailing and secretarial work, than men. Once in work, women are less likely to progress and gain promotion, even in occupations traditionally seen as 'open' such as teaching (NUT/EOC 198). The Civil Service, although making some attempt to increase opportunities for women, has not been notably successful as Table 3.7 indicates:

Table 3.7 Non Industrial Home Civil Service (1980)

	MEN	%	WOMEN
Permanent Secretary	100		0
Under Secretary	95.6		4.4
Principal	92.2		7.8
Executive Officer	62.4		37.6
Clerical Officer	34.1		65.9
Clerical Assistant	20.0		80.0

The rate of increase of unemployment amongst women has increased more rapidly than for men (1977-81 = 97.3% women, 76.3% men). Novarra (1981) makes the point that 'work' is a system made for men by men, thus limiting the opportunities for women to participate fully and equally. Indeed, it is only in times of war that women are actually encouraged to do this, and that facilities such as nurseries are provided to help those with young children fulfill their maternal role as well. This tends to substantiate the Marxist explanation of the sexual division of labour which sees women as a "reserve army of labour", responding to the demands of the capitalist economy.

In conclusion, Hansen (1979) sees five conditions operating to limit the career development of women. We have been examining the power that sex-role conditioning and socialization plays, and referred to the focus on marriage, or its prospect, as key determining factors. She also mentions role conflicts about fulfilling multiple roles in marriage and work, which certainly presents major problems for many women. A lack of work orientation is another factor, and finally, despite legislation, sex discrimination is still practiced. The part that careers officers and teachers can and do play is significant.

A recent EOC study by Benett and Carter (1981) presents a rather mixed picture of the advice and counselling offered to a number of girls. On the one hand, it says that "counselling does take into account the particular abilities and potential of the young person concerned, and that career aspirations of girls are greatly enhanced as a result". However, the case studies do bring out comments like "the teachers just laughed at me", when a girl mentioned an interest in engineering, the bank manager who said "he discourages women from going on day release because they tend to leave and have babies, and break their career", and the careers officer who put a girl off becoming a motor mechanic, because there were many boys who wanted to do this. Rauta and Hunt (1975) found a good deal of dissatisfaction with the careers advice that the girls received, many of them complaining of the limited range of occupations covered.

Finally, Archer and Lloyd (1982) conclude that women are not trying to avoid success at work, but that "stereotypes prescribe the restricted and lower status occupations which are regarded as suitable for women. These beliefs both influence and are derived from differences in educational and vocational training which are available to men and women". Sharpe (1976) adds to this by saying "attitudes, popular ideology and the economic and occupational structure all contribute to girls' inhibitions. Their real opportunities are manipulated by employers (invariably male) who hold the power, wealth and means of production, and have highly reactionary ideas about women and their role; while male employees, who are themselves exploited, hold grimly to the exclusiveness of their skills, backed up by the operation of protective legislation and jobs evaluation".

ETHNIC GROUPS

Another group who need to be considered separately in order to explain their different experiences of work are young blacks. Over the last two decades, three different perspectives to race relations have emerged, and it is worth considering those in order to understand the way in which the 'problem' has been perceived. In the 1950's and 60's, the notion of integration was prominent. This was based on the belief that race relations in Britain were fairly good, and that education should provide cohesion and stability, by means of a curricula that was British. Thus, the emphasis was on playing down the differences between ethnic groups, and concentrating on integrating black children into the British way of life. This perspective can be seen as racist as it defined the 'problem' as being with the black community and assumes the superiority of British culture at the expense of Black culture.

A number of reports and papers have promoted the next perpective, that of diversity. In this case, the specific cultures of various ethnic groups should be taught in schools, and bilingualism encouraged. A low profile on issues of racism and equality is maintained. However, this perspective does lay undue emphasis on culture and tends to ignore the weak position of blacks in the economy and other crucial areas of power. It also lays emphasis on curricula changes rather than practice and the way in which teachers see and treat black pupils.

The last perspective emphasises equality, and has a similar thrust to a feminist view of the position of girls in education. It sees racism as central in British Society, being maintained by the power structure. Discrimination has to be removed from education at all levels. Blacks have to be genuinely consulted and there should be a broad curriculum that tackles issues such as the Third World, as well as other issues like the mass media, for example. As a perspective it argues that racism is contrary to social justice and that it gives both black and white pupils a false view of their own history. It is only in recent years that a good deal of attention has been paid to the educational achievements of black children in this country. In fact, the research has been

> "contradictory, unclear, without any systematic study of factors such as the selective and classificatory processes, teacher attitudes to race and colour, school ethos, or any explanation as to why a number of ethnic minority children are not under-achieving and attaining relatively high results" (Kowalczewski 1982).

Acquiring educational qualifications is obviously an important measure of educational success (and likely occupational success) but other factors have to be considered such as LEA provision and the nature of local communities in order to understand the differences that emerge. Certainly, children of West Indian origin are over-represented in ESN schools, and the Rampton Report (1981) indicated that they do not achieve comparable qualifications to children of white or Asian parents, in schools in general.

Broadly speaking, two sorts of explanation for the underachievement in education (and in employment) of black youngsters have been put forward. The first deals with social-psychological factors such as poor self-image and family background. The second is essentially structural, and focuses on poor provision of educational facilities, plus lack of job opportunities in inner cities, as well as discrimination in employment. Stone (1981) casts doubt on the research that has been carried out on the black self concept; which has tended to describe these self concepts as negative. Weinrach (1979) showed

> "we are all subject to the same psychological pressures which produce our changing self concepts, but that there are special pressures faced by children of ethnic minorities. These differences result from their position in the wider society, and not, as it is often assumed, from problems inherent in the minority populations. Conflicts in identification are valuable and normal resources, not the peculiar liabilities of immigrant children".

Certainly the factor of black children being only partly educated in this country has now largely disappeared, so differences in attainment have to be explained in other ways. Bilingualism is still a 'problem', but it is one that has been present for a long time and is true for other minority groups, e.g. Welsh, Poles, etc., who, in fact achieve more educationally. For some years, the West Indian Community have tried to counter 'inadequate' state schooling by organising their own supplementary or Saturday schools, which teach in a more formal manner, and include Black studies in their curriculum.

In 1981, the interim report of the Committee, chaired by Anthony Rampton, published its findings on West Indian children in British Schools. A D.E.S. survey (1978/9) of 1403 black pupls (527 Asian, 799 West Indian) and 4,852 white pupils, leaving school, produced the following statistical evidence for the report. For English C.S.E. and 'O' level, 9% West Indian, 21% Asian, and 29% white children, obtained higher grades. For mathematics, the figures were 5% West Indian, 20% Asian, and 19% white pupils. All C.S.E. and 'O' level (5 or more higher grades) - 3% West Indian, 18% Asian, and 16% white pupils. Entry to University was 1% West Indian, 3% Asian, 3% white pupils.

In its conclusions the report identified unintentional racism in schools, which took the form of stereotyped or patronising attitudes to West Indian children. It was felt that explicit racism was very much in the minority. However, racism alone could not account for the underachievement of West Indian children, neither was much weight given to linguistic difficulties. The curriculum and the examination system needs to adopt a multi-cultural approach. Likewise, a "Gulf in trust and understanding" between West Indian parents and teachers was seen as an important contributory factor, and in service and initial training needs to tackle this issue.

In looking at the employment opportunities for black youngsters, it is worth considering a widely accepted dual labour market theory. Black workers and women are seen as being socialised into the secondary sector, with its poorer jobs, conditions, opportunities, training and pay, whilst white men are concentrated in the primary sector, which offers better conditions, etc. There have been a number of comparative studies of young black and white workers, and it is proposed to see how far these empirical studies support this theory. One study by Dex (1982) traced the employment experience of a group of black and white school leavers from Birmingham and London, between 1971 and 1976. Black youths valued work for its intrinsic meaning more than white youths. Careers Officers seemed to have lower expectations of the black youths as did employers, which meant that they were behind whites in the labour queue; one apparent response by these black youths was to take further education courses. It was notable that the black youths had broken away from potentially dominated "black industries" and that they used the Careers Service more extensively than white youths. Once in their first job, they used black contacts more, and the Careers Service less, in order to change jobs.

The women in the survey regarded their role in paid employment as significant and a source of potential happiness, although, unlike the boys, the emphasis was less on pay, and more on work as a source of meeting people. Work sought was largely traditional, e.g. clerical. Black girls were less successful in obtaining jobs they wanted, and like the boys, they used the Careers service more than whites in finding their first job. Certainly racial discrimination played a part in their job hunting, and this may account for their tendency to drop out of the labour market for a while. Black girls displayed a similar keeness to enter further education and undergo training.

Many of these observations were confirmed in a study of various ethnic school leavers in Bradford and Sheffield in 1972, (Allen and Smith, 1975). It was a comprehensive study which involved the youngsters being interviewed twice, as well as teachers, careers officers and employers being contacted. Pupils of Asian and West Indian origin were not expected to do as well as white pupils, by their schools, and racial sterotyping was evident. This was apparent as far as getting a job was concerned; lack of success was attributed to individual failure. Stereotyping was also apparent as regards girls and the sorts of jobs they were expected to enter. With regard to the Youth Employment Service, nearly all the sample had been interviewed, but over half felt that the Service had not been useful to them. Allen and Smith make the point that the parents of these black pupils, as immigrants, occupied jobs in the secondary labour market. There is a widespread expectation that their children will do the same, but not amongst the black pupils themselves. The fact that they did not enter jobs in the primary sector to the same extent as white males is an indication of this expectation working in practice.

A more recent study (Roberts, Duggan and Noble, 1981) also compared the experiences of a group of black and white teenagers in six multi-racial inner city areas. Most had left at 16, with few qualifications, and all were disadvantaged in terms of their social origins. There was a direct relationship between skin colour, qualifications, gender and unemployment. Thus, unqualified black girls were likely to have spent five times as much time unemployed as qualified white boys. Roberts et al point out that ethnic differences exist, although both black and white girls are disadvantaged. For instance, white girls are more likely to leave the labour market when they become mothers, as opposed to black girls in the same position.

Although pupils of West Indian origin underachieve in Britain as a whole, they achieved greater success than the white youngsters in this sample. In fact, black youngsters entered the same sorts of jobs as white youngsters, but it took them longer to do this. Blacks were at a disadvantage however, by not having parents who could 'pull strings' to enter skilled jobs. Black youngsters used the statutory employment services as much as whites and found them useful. There was a high rate of job changing, especially by blacks, who were thus exposed to a greater risk of unemployment. Young blacks were more ambitious than whites, even allowing for their higher qualifications, but their expectations were not 'unrealistically' high. Black men wanted skilled manual jobs, whilst the girls wanted office work. As with other studies, blacks were more likely to have received some further education.

Roberts et al point out that blacks seem "unrealistically ambitious only within inner cities, where teachers and careers officers are accustomed to compliant school leavers expressing willingness to consider any job that pays anything above the dole". Black parents are anxious for their children to avoid the sorts of poor jobs that they have occupied. Black youngsters reject these jobs as 'rubbish work' and 'slave labour'. The crucial problem is the lack of availability of better jobs in the inner cities. Aspiring white families are more likely to move (and be able to) to areas of better employment. Black families are equivocal about leaving known people and places which provide some security for them. Therefore black youngsters find it hard to reconcile themselves to 'slave labour' and accordingly turn to 'hustling' or learning to survive on casual earnings, social security and support from friends and family. A very recent survey of 16-20 year olds, conducted by the Opinion Research Centre for the Commission for Racial Equality showed the following figures:

Table 3.8

	EDUCATION	WORK (all as %)	UNEMPLOYED
Afro-Caribbeans	36	24	36
Asians	45	31	21
Whites	26	42	30

Finally, it is worth noting that the Rampton Committee (1981) identified careers education and advice as having unduly low expectations of West Indian pupils at times and when linked to discrimination in employment, this had a demotivating effect.

SOCIOLOGICAL EXPLANATIONS OF OCCUPATIONAL CHOICE

Opportunity Structure

In the last decade, Ken Roberts (1968, 1971, 1977) has made a notable contribution to a sociological understanding of occupational choice. He has focussed attention away from the individual choice towards the social structures significant to the individual's entry to employment. Hence he describes his theory in terms of 'opportunity structure'. The theory is based on the following assertions:

1.)Neither school leavers nor adults typically choose their jobs in any meaningful sense; they simply take what is available. Job preferences are not mere matters of individual taste but are determined by a system of stratification.

2.)The occupational opportunities open to any school leaver are structured by a number of factors, the most important of which is that the individual's educational attainments and his freedom of occupational choice are really strictly limited.

3.)School leavers stand in varying degrees of social proximity to different types of occupations. These varying degrees of social proximity have nothing to do with the ambitions of the individuals concerned. They are inherent in the structure of the educational institutions that the young people are leaving and the occupational institutions they are entering.

Thus Roberts maintains, that for all individuals, whatever their qualifications, the social structure determines their eventual occupation. He points to socialization creating a climate of expectation which is associated with particular educational careers, and internalised by each individual. Their aspirations are the result of anticipatory socialization, which takes place first in the family, with most children learning traditional sex roles, and values related to work. This is put into graphic terms by Gross (1958) when he stated that "it makes a difference to a child's ambition pattern whether the voices from the living room, that he listens to in bed (when he should be asleep) are those of successful lawyers or successful pickpockets".

Roberts is, in fact, following the sociological tradition of conceptualising occupational entry in terms of selection, allocation and placement. However, he does pose some crucial questions concerning the belief that individuals choose their occupations, and the apparent acquiescence of so many individuals who enter poorly paid and boring jobs (or have no jobs at all). Inevitably, the answer lies in the process of socialization, which adjusts the expectations and aspirations of individuals by means of gender roles, ethnic stereotyping, and social class images within the family, the education system, and the media.

Roberts' work is of particular interest because he discusses the role of the Careers Service at some length. For instance, he says that "irrespective of their sincerity, careers workers cannot simply help young people towards self-understanding and jobs, in which they will optimise their own values. Career workers either direct young people towards jobs they are structurally obliged to enter, in which case they are objectively acting as part of the social control apparatus, or they encourage young people to develop aims that discord with the opportunities they eventually encounter. In the latter event, this radical cultural work may one day help to precipitate structural change. Alternatively, it might simply leave young people maladjusted to the occupations they are pragmatically obliged to enter". Careers work cannot be neutral.

There is an element of determinism in Roberts' work on occupational choice that can be disconcerting to those working in vocational guidance. He seems to be saying that the structural constraints are such that individuals have no real choice, hence vocational guidance is largely an illusion. Certainly, he advocates careers officers moving away from a developmental role, based on careers education and adopting the role of placement officer (Roberts, 1977). This has been strongly contested by Daws (1977), with some success. However, in recent years, unemployment has strengthened Roberts's arguments, and the growing number of unemployment specialist careers officers are fulfilling the sort of role he advocated.

Daws (1977) does provide a powerful critique of Roberts' opportunity structure theory. Firstly, he questions whether it can be described as a theory, as Roberts himself has suggested that it will not fit all situations, thus weakening its comprehensiveness. Secondly, Daws maintains that Roberts does not take into account the rapidity of contemporary, social and economic change, and with it, the degree of social mobility. Thirdly, Daws feels that Roberts denies the value of psychological theories of occupational choice, without sufficient evidence. Daws sees a place for both disciplines in providing a comprehensive explanation of occupational choice.

Roberts makes an eloquent and persuasive case for his opportunity structure perspective. However, if his own empirical evidence is examined, this is found to be lacking. His original study (1968) was based on a survey of 196 men aged 14 to 23 in a London Borough in 1965. There is information lacking on this sample, for instance, ethnic background, educational qualifications, social class. It is also notable that women were not included. In order to present a theory as positively as Roberts does, a much sounder empirical base is required.

AN INTERDISCIPLINARY FRAMEWORK

The conceptual framework of Blau et al (1956) has a number of advantages. It combines a developmental perspective with a structural approach. It emphasises the compromises that take place in both choice and entry, and makes clear the diversity of influences that play a part in determining the occupational choice of any individual.

Figure 3.9 Occupational Choice - a conceptual framework

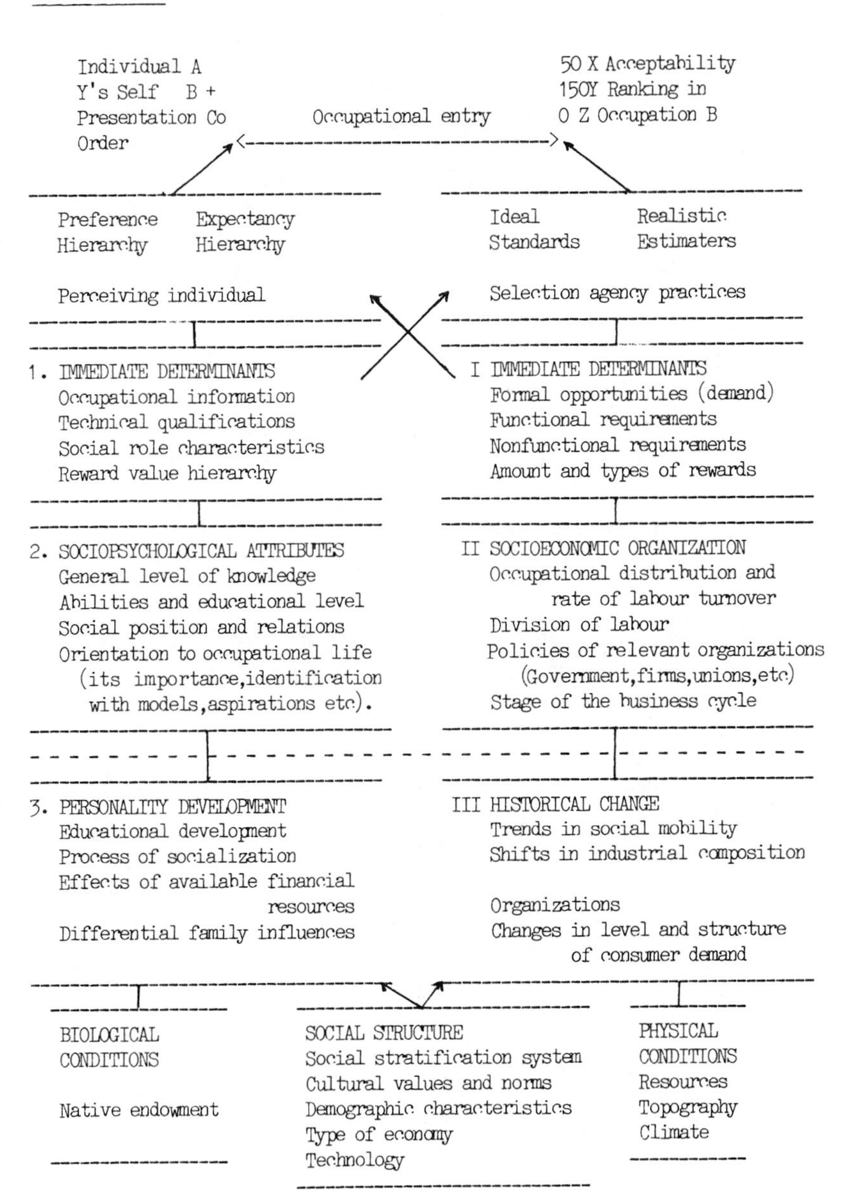

Schema of the process of occupational choice and selection

The framework requires some clarification and discussion. The left hand column represents the development of the individual from birth, at the bottom of the framework, to the top which represents the moment of occupational entry (not choice). The right hand column describes a similar sort of developmental process, although over a longer period, describing how circumstances have arisen that certain employers are (or are not) recruiting for jobs at the same moment, as the individual is seeking employment. The social structure, bottom centre of the framework has dual significance. It influences the personality development of the choosers, and it defines the socioeconomic conditions in which selection takes place. Blau et al point out, however, the individual makes decisions affected by the past social structure, whereas occupational opportunities are determined by the present structure. Therefore, a young man or woman could have pursued their studies, in say, chemistry to post-doctoral level on the understanding that this would gain them entry into industrial research, only to find the recession had made this well nigh impossible.

The left hand side of the model traces individual development from initial biological conditions, which presumably covers a number of factors, including gender and skin colour. "Biological potentialities are transformed into personality traits" by means of family, peers, teachers, the community and the media. Above the broken line, sociopsychological attributes have an immediate bearing upon occupational choice. Thus the educational level achieved, and the sorts of abilities demonstrated, will combine with social class background, and the level of aspiration and motivation to determine the occupational decisions made. These decisions, although cumulative, are usually near to the point of leaving full-time education.

At this moment, the four factors in Box 1 are crucial. Occupational information is accepted as meaning details of vacancies, more general information about types of work and actual advice, and counselling. Technical qualifications refers to the sorts of qualifications achieved, whilst social role, characteristics refers to the host of factors such as gender, dress, speech, manner, etc., which, in turn, is linked to reward value hierarchy. This denotes the individual's priorities in relation to work, e.g. money, travel, working with the hands, status, etc.

These immediate factors correspond to those in Box 1. Formal opportunities are reflected in the actual demand by employers for workers, and the sorts of workers required. Functional requirements are stated in terms of qualifications needed, physical attributes, psychological qualities, working experience etc. Some of these apparently functional requirements may indeed be non-functional, i.e. not really essential to perform the job adequately. For example, the "attractive" physical attributes said to be essential by the Kansas City television station, for its female newscasters, was ruled to be discriminating by a Federal jury, in the case brought by a sacked woman newscaster (Guardian 10.8.83).

Many non-functional requirements have been used explicitly by employers in the past to restrict entry to certain jobs, e.g. gender, colour, type of school attended, etc. In recent years, this has either been ruled illegal, or has become overt. However, there is much evidence to suggest that these non-functional requirements still exist, and play an important part in restricting entry to a range of occupations. High unemployment makes it easier for employers to discriminate unfairly. How careers officers and teachers respond to this situation is an important question, as young people need support in countering sexism, racism, bias against handicaps, and class bias. However, it must be said that some of those engaged in vocational guidance are likely to subscribe to the same values of those employers who discriminate unfairly, thus undermining this support. This sort of selection on non-functional grounds is difficult to prove, and could be said to apply equally to "over selection", on the basis of educational qualifications.

Box 2 covers less immediate, but no less important factors. The geographical distribution of occupations is crucial, and the rate of labour turnover clearly effects the availability of jobs. The actual division of labour changes, as a result of technology and other factors, has created a relative increase in white collar jobs, and a decrease in manual occupations, in recent years. Policies of government, employers, and trade unions, all play a part in the changing nature of the occupational structure. The notion of the business cycle, with booms and slumps, is all too familiar a factor in influencing the availability of employment. Finally, the remaining two boxes both play longer term roles, in influencing the nature of the occupational structure.

Occupational entry is the culmination of the individual's occupational choice and the selection decisions made by employers. The individual compromises his ideal preference of job, based on previous rejections, and his expectation of success or failure. Equally, the employer has certain ideal standards established for his vacancies, but will alter these upwards or downwards, depending on the availability of applicants. In conclusion, Blau et al stress the point that occupational choice is a series of inter-related decisions, rather that a single choice. Clearly a number of these decisions are not actually made by the individual, and are irreversible. The framework, although clearly expressed, does illustrate the point that occupational choice and entry is not just complex, but also subject to changing circumstances. Social science does offer the possibility of both studying the process, and keeping abreast of change.

CONCLUSION

There is a great deal of evidence to support the view that occupational choice is a complex process. Indeed, there is a danger, at one extreme of over-complicating its analysis, or at the other extreme, of reacting by oversimplyfying occupational choice. The following model attempts to steer a middle course. As a model, it does not offer any prediction of occupational choice, but focuses on the key processes. The model operates on two levels. Firstly, there are five primary factors that play the major role in determining occupational choice, and operate developmentally from birth, through to adulthood. Secondly, there are three secondary factors that operate for the most part, from the age of five onwards. All these eight factors can be seen to influence occupational choice and occupational entry on a 'enabling-disabling' scale.

SOCIOLOGICAL EXPLANATIONS FOR OCCUPATIONAL CHOICE

PRIMARY FACTORS

These are all of key importance in determining occupational choice, and it is not possible to rank them in any significant order.

1. Socio-Economic Class

Sociologists use father's occupation to classify social class, but this sort of classification presents increasing problems with high levels of male unemployment, plus an increasing number of children being brought up solely by their mothers. Even in families with father working, and mother either in paid employment or at home, the mother's present or past job will be of significance. The occupations of both parents play an important part in determining the occupational choices of their children. This is made clear from the discussion of a wide variety of research earlier in this chapter.

2. Gender

Men and women's roles are still perceived differently, and this has a direct influence upon their preparation for work. This begins in the family, continues in all levels of education, and is confirmed at work. Equal opportunities legislation has had some impact, but change has been slow, and the current recession is likely to halt, or indeed reverse this change.

3. Ethnic Origin

Britain is a multi-racial society with a significant number of minority groups, who present a somewhat confusing picture. For instance, the evidence strongly supports the view that youngster of Afro-Carribbean origin underachieve in education and at work, whilst this does not seem to be true, to the same extent, for youngsters of Asian origin. However, there is no doubt that ethnic origin is an important factor, although more complex, than social class or gender.

4. Physical Characteristics.

This refers to a wide variety of factors. Obviously, those youngsters who have some severe physical disability, such as blindness, are going to be restricted in their occupational choice. Likewise, certain sorts of physiques are necessary to enter particular occupations, e.g. police, jockey. Similarly there are certain minor disabilities that are commonplace but eliminate some occupations, e.g. poor eyesight - pilot. Thus, some physical characteristics are enabling, and help to draw an individual to a particular occupation, whilst other physical characteristics are disabling, and limit occupational choice.

5. Level of Intelligence

Intelligence, rather than attainment, was chosen as a primary factor. Attainments are often crucial in determining occupational entry, and in narrowing down occupational choice. Certainly, a considerable number of people do not reach the level of attainment of which they are capable, especially at school. In recent years, it has become more feasible to attain qualifications as mature students, and these opportunities have been readily taken up, particularly by women. This has sometimes led to significant changes of occupation in later life.

It is probably self-evident how these five factors act to enable or disable the individual's occupational choice. Only the first factor, socio-economic class is a strictly social factor, in contrast to the other four which all have a biological base. In no respect is this suggesting that occupational choice is biologically determined. On the contrary, it is clear that a factor like gender, whilst based on some biological differences, becomes particularly important in occupational choice and entry, when socially constructed differences operate. For example, the differences in physical strength between men and women is much less important occupationally, than the notion that "the woman's place is in the home". Thus, being a man tends to be an enabling factor, whilst being a woman tends to be a disabling factor.

Secondary Factors.

These three factors become more important nearer to the actual time of occupational choice and entry.

1. Educational Experience.

The individual's overall experience within the educational system is going to be significant in a host of different ways. Teacher expectations of attainment and occupational choice, the quality of facilities available, the curriculum, whether the school is private or state funded, selective or non-selective; the list is a long one. Early, as well as later, experience of education plays a part in forming attitudes towards work. The most tangible result of education is qualifications or lack of them, but the hidden 'curriculum' must also be considered.

2. Exposure to Occupational Information, and Vocational Guidance.

Each of us are continuously exposed to images of people at work from an early age. Some of these images are literally close to home, in terms of family occupations, others are transmitted by the media and education. These images vary in their potency, but they tend to establish and preserve certain sterotypes of work, i.e. bricklayers are men, M.P.'s are white, solicitors are middle class. It is difficult to break away from these stereotypes, especially if they are subscribed to by 'significant others', i.e. peers, teachers, parents, etc. Some of this exposure may be direct through part-time jobs or work experience schemes. Careers education and vocational guidance can play an important part in influencing both occupational choice and entry, although this can be overestimated.

3. Availability of Employment

The occupational structure, in terms of the range and number of jobs available, plays a significant part in occupational choice in two respects. Firstly, the local labour market, in particular, will help form most peoples' expectations of the type of work they might hope to enter. Secondly, when it is time to get a job, the actual availability of work will largely determine the sort of job each individual enters. This may not be a 'real' job, but a place on a training scheme. In some areas unemployment, rather than employment, has dominated the local community, and this will have a pervasive influence upon occupational thinking.

The model lays emphasis on sociological, rather than psychological factors, although there is an underlying assumption of an interaction between the individual psyche, and the surrounding society. This emphasis is intended to right the balance, which has tended to view occupational choice in terms of essentially internally motivated needs, traits or personality types. Certainly any theory that is likely to offer a comprehensive explanation of occupational choice will have to draw upon both psychology and sociology. A satisfactory theory of occupational choice has to fulfill two criteria. Firstly, it must take into consideration the crucial structural influences that have a major impact on the life chances of all individuals. Secondly, it must be able to account for individual differences that occur which cannot be fully explained by these structural influences.

Chapter Four

THE INTERVIEW

"To get or to give or to be?" Gilbert Wrenn

Despite the recent growth of computer based guidance systems and the much longer history of psychological testing, the interview has remained the "corner stone" of vocational guidance practice. From the pioneering days of Frank Parsons, it has been seen as the focus, indeed the culmination of the process of vocational guidance. The interview comes in many shapes and forms and this chapter will explore its various dimensions.

The interview has often been attacked as being, in some sense, artificial and therefore an inferior experience. This is not inevitable. Indeed Benjamin (1969) describes the interview as "a conversation between two people, a conversation that is serious and purposeful." Hence the interview can be seen as being in the mainstream of normal communication and in fact, a good deal has been learnt about the interpersonal communication from research work in this field.

It is necessary to examine the theoretical basis of the interview before actually looking in detail at the way vocational interviews are conducted. Farr (1982) states that "there is, at present, no adequate theory in psychology of direct relevance to the practice of interviewing." He suggests a number of criteria for an adequate theory of the interview. For instance, it must also be a theory of the human self and it must take into account states of awareness or consciousness in the parties to the interaction.

Farr draws upon the work of a number of writers in seeking a theory of the interview. Heider is one of these and it is his work on the psychology of interpersonal relations that is especially relevant. Man becomes particularly aware that what others know about him is conjectural, when he is interviewed. The act of being observed leads to certain actions. Goffman sees this in terms of the participants as actors on stage; the experience leading to 'impression management'. The concept of the mirror is important with both the actor or the interviewee using it to become an 'object' to themselves.

Thus the interview is a highly 'reactive' way of appraising people as the process actually alters what is being observed. This conclusion lead some psychologists to reject the interview in favour of psychological testing, which was seen as a much more scientific and objective method of appraisal. The rejection has perhaps diverted psychologists from seeking to improve the interview, although as we shall see later in this chapter the aims and objectives of the interview can be such as to render this assessment largely irrelevant.

G.H. Mead, the American philosopher was much concerned with developing a theory of the Self. Man according to Mead is self reflexive, in other words, self aware. He can thus act towards himself as an object, but he can also assume the role of the other. In this way he can engage himself in interaction, by means of an internalised dialogue. In relation to the interview, this means that man reacts to his own actions, on the basis of the actual or the anticipated reactions to others. The notion of role playing and role reversal are now well established methods of interview training and self awareness exercises.

Later in the chapter, a variety of approaches to vocational counselling will be considered. These approaches illustrate how the major theoretical positions in psychology influence the practice of vocational guidance and counselling in radically different ways. Each has a slightly different model of man, and therefore make different assumptions about the process of occupational choice.

<u>Philosophy</u>

Anyone working in the field of vocational guidance and counselling should examine the 'philosophy' that lies behind the way in which they interview. Benjamin states that

> "at best, the helping interview will provide the interviewee with a meaningful experience

> leading to change. The experience is the relationship with you; change is what hopefully results from this relationship; a change in his ideas, a change in his feelings about himself and others, a change in the information he possesses about a topic important to him - a change in himself as a person".

He goes on to pose some important questions about the interviewer's need to be needed and the client's need to have control of his own life and to become independent as soon as possible.

Benjamin talks about creating an atmosphere of trust, and showing the client that we consider him responsible for his actions and that we believe in him using his own resources. He goes on to say

> "we do not tell him what to think or how to feel, but our behaviour reveals that we value thoughts and feelings, our own and his. It indicates that the more he can discover about his own, the more he will be able to act upon them or modify them, should he so choose. We wish to help him come closer to himself and thereby to others."

This may suggest that the interviewer should assume a passive role, but far from it. Although the interviewer may not talk a great deal, he should be active in gaining a deep understanding of the client and his world, by his prescence and interest. In no sense should the interviewer neglect his authority but he should use it to put the client in the centre of the stage, thus enabling him to look more deeply at himself.

The interviewer should not seek to make decisions for his client, thus taking away his capacity to learn and become responsible. Ultimately the interviewer brings himself to the interview and it is the quality of the relationship that he is able to make with the client that matters. Honesty and openness are qualities that the interviewer seeks from his client and he must offer these in return. Showing respect for the client is an essential part of establishing an open relationship between interviewer and client. This can be shown in practical ways. For instance, by waiting for a client to finish what he wants to say rather than cutting in and trying to extract some information that the interviewer feels is necessary. Acceptance is another key area and this means treating the client as an equal by respecting his right to ideas and opinions which may sometimes run quite contrary to the interviewer's. It may be that it is not possible to accept some clients and in these cases, it is better for all concerned to find another interviewer. In such cases, the interview ceases to be a helping interview.

Understanding is clearly at the heart of any helping interview. Benjamin suggests that there are three ways of understanding. Firstly, there is the understanding about the client, based upon secondhand information, from his school for instance. This can be helpful and is often regarded as objective, if it emanates from an 'official source'. However, it is inevitably going to be a distorted understanding of that individual. Secondly, the interviewer seeks to understand the client through his own eyes, ears,feelings and knowledge. This understanding, although closer to the client than the first sort of understanding, is still in terms of the interviewer's experience, values and attitudes. This puts a limitation on the extent to which the interviewer can really understand his client, which brings us to the third sort of understanding; understanding with the client. To quote Benjamin

> "this calls for putting everything aside, everything but our own common humanness and with it alone trying to understand with the other person how he thinks, feels and sees the world about him. It means ridding ourselves of our internal frame of reference and adopting his. Here, the issue is not to disagree or agree with him, but to understand what it is like to be him. Seemingly quite simple, though in reality difficult to achieve."

This level of understanding is intimately linked with active and effective listening. By this is meant, listening that is not diminished by the interviewer's preoccupation with what his is going to say next. It is listening not just to what is being said, but to how it is said, the non-verbal communication that goes with the words, and, finally, what is not said. It should be a total process which involves the interviewer's ears, eyes, mind and heart. There is a paradox with this sort of involvement. It is that the interviewer becomes so absorbed with the client's frame of reference that he is no longer in touch with his own frame of reference and thus becomes less effective in helping the client see certain important things about himself.

The term 'empathy' must be introduced at this point. It is not the same as sympathy which is sharing common feelings, nor is it like identification, which is wishing to be like the other person. It is caring for the client sufficiently to want to learn about him by temporarily abandoning one's own lifespace. By demonstrating empathy towards the client, the interviewer can increase his level of understanding of that client and will communicate a genuine concern for his needs.

Carl Rogers (1978) has pointed out that our need to evaluate, to confirm or to deny, provides a real block to good communication. This is sometimes a result of the interviewer's desire to reassure the client. For instance, a client may express a fear of selection interviews. A careers officer might respond by saying that there is really nothing to worry about, because the client is well qualified and is sure to get a job soon. This would, in fact, be a denial of the client's feelings and not reassuring. It is likely to make the client hesitant to make another comment of a similar nature as this may lead to a further 'denial'.

The interviewer, by virtue of his role, has a certain authority. How he chooses to use this authority is crucial. If he chooses to hide behind it, using is as a defence, this will inhibit the interview. When the interviewer approaches his client with a sense of equality, communication is likely to improve. The client will begin to see the person behind the role, someone who is human and fallible like himself, someone who does not possess all the answers, but someone who is real.

Structure

In the course of time, many interviewers tend to forget the importance of how they open interviews. This is probably connected with a concern to move quickly to the main body of the interview, which is understandably seen as the focus of the exercise. This is a mistake, as the client needs to be initiated into the interview before it begins in earnest. How the interviewer opens any interview will depend on who initiated is in the first place. If the client has sought the interview, the interviewer should put any assumptions on one side and let the client state freely why he has requested to see him. There is no need for the interviewer to say much; it is better to give the client space to state what he wants from the interviewer in his own words, and, at his own pace.

Many vocational guidance interviews are arranged for the client by the School. The client will come with some knowledge and expectation of the interview, although both of these may be erroneous. The interviewer should be brief in his introduction, and, at all cost, avoid the interview becoming a monologue or a lecture. The introduction should include some mention of the interviewer's role, if this has not been explained to the client beforehand, by means of a talk or a handout. It is also better to avoid spelling out the structure of the remaining interview too much, as the client is likely to feel constrained and possibly limited by this. First impressions are often regarded as very influential in human relations, and equally the opening of any interview sets the tone for the remainder of the interchange.

Some very powerful messages can be transmitted consciously and unconsciously by the interviewer, at this early stage, and it is as well to be aware of these messages and their consequences. For instance, the interviewer who opens the interview by talking for the first few minutes, setting out in detail what he wants from the interview is likely to give the client the impression that, he, the interviewer, is 'running the interview' and, he, the client, is there to be questioned, sized up and labelled. On the other hand, the interviewer who makes it plain to the client that the interview is for him, the client, to use as he sees fit is likely to encourage a more positive and participative response. Indeed, it may be in the interests of both parties to establish a "contract' at the start of the interview, whereby interviewer and client broadly agree on the use of time and the conduct of the interview, and perhaps beyond the interview itself.

Intimately connected with the matter of the opening of the interview are its actual objectives or goals. Wicks (1982) suggests that the following are some of the goals of Vocational Guidance

- self appraisal, equipping the client to achieve realistic self assessement.

- self perception, providing frames for reference, categories of occupationally significant behaviours.

- job perception, acquiring the skills required to assess the world of work in terms of job content, values, roles and life styles.

- reality testing, matching aspirations and goals with opportunities within one's limitations.

- setting goals and objectives, specifying obtainable goals and precise objectives.

- hypothesis generation, helping the client to generate occupational 'theories'.

- interaction of the person and the job environment, examining the complexities of the person/work situation interaction.

- sharing information, providing the client with educational and occupational information, and providing the counsellor with perceptions of the client.

- task setting, translating immediate goals into discrete tasks such as finding an address, seeking information, reading a pamphlet, etc.

This formidable list is beyond the scope of a single interview or even possibly a series of interviews. Thus the interviewer must make a number of decisions. He must first decide how far,or if at all, he is going to outline the goals of the interview. If he does plan to outline the goals, how much detail does he enter into, what does he mention, and what does he exclude?

THE INTERVIEW

Questions

It is easy for those new to interviewing to see the process as largely one of question and answer. Certainly a lot of attention is devoted to the nature and type of questions used by interviewers and rightly so. However, it is important to consider the actual role of the question and how it affects the nature of the interview. Benjamin (1969) feels that a pattern of question and answer can soon be established in an interview that will be difficult to break out of. The client will adopt a passive role, that of an object, and with this, a number of expectations will arise. He will expect the interviewer to use all this information he is collecting in some meaningful and 'expert' fashion to 'solve' his problem. Too many questions can turn the interview into an interrogation, whereas very often it is not necessary to ask so many questions. A few open questions will allow the client to talk about the things that are important to him and the interviewer may only need to prompt him from time to time. It is also true to say that if the interviewer is too preoccupied with thinking about the next question, he will be giving insufficient attention to what the client is saying.

The open question is broad, allowing the client full scope. It invites him to express his views, opinions, thoughts, feelings and aims, to deepen the contact between client and interviewer. Therefore the question "Can you tell me how you feel about school?" is likely to elicit a fuller, richer answer that "Do you like school?" Likewise, the indirect question helps to create a freer atmosphere in the interview, with the client feeling less cross questioned. An example of this could relate to the issue of unemployment. Instead of saying "do you think you're going to find it difficult to get a job when you leave school?", the interviewer could introduce the topic by saying "Getting a job in this area is quite a problem."

Benjamin is critical of the double question posing an 'either/or' choice. The question "Do you want to leave school and get a job, or stay on?", does not lead very far. It might be more productive to say "How far have you got in deciding what you're going to do at the end of this year?" Certainly another problem centres around asking too many questions too rapidly. Many young clients need time to adjust to the interview situation and are likely to respond to direct, closed or leading questions with the minimum response. This puts pressure on the interviewer to ask yet more questions in order to 'fill the space' left by the client. Anxiety felt by the interviewer is likely to transmit itself to the client, and lead to a spiral of more and more limited communication and growing frustration.

Questions that start with the word 'Why' come in for particular criticism from Benjamin. He maintains that although the word was once employed to seek information, it now has connotations of disapproval. This connotation can be transmitted without the intention of the interviewer, but the effect upon the client can still be negative. Hence the question "Why don't you like maths?", although asked without any implied blame, may not strike the client in the same way. He will probably be used to being questioned at school with regard to his behaviour or performance, and this sort of question will merely fall into the category of 'an adult in authority putting me on the spot'. A suitably evasive answer may well follow. The client will feel the need to defend himself and will consequently close, rather than open up.

It is worth exploring this facet of questioning further, as it does highlight the relationship between interviewer and client. Benjamin states that

> "the 'why' seems to demand of the interviewer an answer that he may not possess, one that is unclear to him or one that he is not willing to share - at least not yet, perhaps because of the way the interviewer is going about obtaining it."

Asking 'why' is often easier than finding another way of broaching the same matter. In fact, by saying "I see you say that you don't like Maths", may well be sufficient to get the client talking about the subject.

Interviewers need to look closely at the questions they ask, because it is easy to get into a pattern without realising it. Often it is only by listening to recordings or by the comments of an observer that we realise our mistakes. What seemed to be a useful question can, on examination, have been non-productive or even negative. There is evidence that a number of professional groups do not vary their style of questioning to accomodate different clients.

Reddy and Brannigan (1982) have done some detailed research on Careers Officers' interviews. Amongst other things, this focused on questions, statements and responses made by both interviwers and clients. Interviewers made, on average, in each interview, 39 statments, 19 closed questions, 11 open questions, 2 double questions and 12 leading questions. Clients made 9 statements, asked 1 closed question, each interview, but responded as asked 38 times as opposed to responding not as asked 4 times per interview. Such blanket figures give only a general indication of the pattern of question and response, but they do serve to show a tendency to ask closed or leading questions, as opposed to open questions. The preponderance of statements, i.e. one every forty seconds or the interview, is difficult to judge without examining the nature of the statements. However, occupational information occupied a high proportion of the content of the interview, so it it fair to assume that a lot of these statements were associated with this topic. The frequency of questions, asked by Careers Officers was one every thirty six seconds of the interview, which suggests a high level of questioning and relatively short responses by clients.

Talking

The term 'inter-view' suggests an exchange between client and interviewer. Verbal exchanges form the significant part of the interview and how 'talk time' is actually shared is an important issue in vocational guidance. Reddy and Brannigan's recent study of 29 Careers Officers (1982), interviewing 114 clients, produced some interesting findings. Careers Officers occupied 69.8% of 'Talk Time' as opposed to 25.4% occupied by their clients; the remaining time being silence. They conclude that "the interviews analysed represent a picture biased in favour of the interviewer who, if talkativeness, introduction of topic, questionning, can be taken as measures, 'controls' or 'directs' the interaction".

Benjamin (1969) says that

> "if you tend to talk as much or even more than the interviewee, chances are that you are blocking communication from him to you. It is quite likely that you are acting as an authority, as the superior in the interview who must be respectfully listened to, and that the interviewee perceives you in this way. You may be lecturing the interviewee and not becoming sufficiently aware of this internal frame of reference while causing him to become too much aware of yours".

The Careers Officer or teacher can certainly be perceived as an 'authority figure', as someone occupying an official position, and with access to information and valuable knowledge. This puts an onus on him to talk and for the client to listen, which no doubt helps to account for Reddy and Brannigan's findings, in part at least. However, to return to Benjamin, it is also true to say that "our need to talk, unfortunately, is often greater than our ability to listen. This is a very human failing, but since it creates obstacles to communication, it should be overcome."

Concern with one's role is something that can absorb the attention of the interviewer to the extent that he may not be listening to the client fully. This is a common fault with interviewers who are over concerned with the structure of their interviews and perhaps with the impression they are creating. The interviewer should be aiming to respond naturally and directly with the client which he can only do by listening to his client, rather than thinking about the next question. Preoccupation with self is a common problem with trainee interviewers; and is something that can be dealt with in training to some degree. This is more likely to be true when the training is not just concerned with skills, but also give attention to the experiential side of human relations training.

It is certainly true that some clients seem prepared to say very little in interviews and this can present a problem to the interviewer (although this may suit some very well!). The interviewer is tempted on these occasions to fill the 'vacuum' created by the silent client by talking. This may succeed by encouraging the client, but it may have just the opposite effect, of demonstrating that if the client doesn't say anything, the interviewer will! The interviewer may need to give the client space to talk by being silent himself. This is not a 'game' to see who can keep quiet longest but a way of saying to the client that the interviewer is prepared to wait for him to speak and not rush him into saying something. If this fails, it may be necessary to confront the client with his silence.

Some clients have been sent to be interviewed by parents or school and are unwilling, or unready for the experience. This leads to their silence or lack of response. The interviewer needs to discover this, and it may be necessary to terminate or abbreviate the interview, as nothing worthwhile is likely to come from it. This can be done in such a way that the client will be prepared to come and see the interviewer in the future, when he feels ready.

Silence

However, in considering questioning and talking, it is necessary to look at certain other aspects of the interview, and silence is one of these aspects. At first, this may seem strange as silence might appear to have little place or importance in the interview. Indeed, those new to interviewing usually regard silences as a waste of valuable time and something to be guarded against. Silences are seen as embarrassing pauses in communication, which should be ended as quickly as possible by the interviewer. This is a common misunderstanding of the function of silence, which can in fact be most productive, if used sensitively. In fact, it is interesting to note that Reddy and Brannigan (1982) found few Careers Officers using silence in their interviews. Silence took up 5.3% of interview time; 4.2% after the Careers Officer had spoken, and 1.1% after the client had spoken. This last figure supports their contention that "Careers Officers do not remain silent after a client has spoken in the expectation that further information could be elicited in this way".

Silence serves a number of functions. Quite simply, the client may need time to sort out his thoughts and feelings, and the interviewer should respect this need. By waiting, it is likely that the client will respond to the interviewer in a clearer, more thoughtful manner and perhaps make a subsequent question unnecessary. Silences sometimes arise because the client, or occasionally the interviewer has not understood what the other person has said. Where confusion has arisen, the shorter the silence the better.

Silence can sometimes be seen as resistance on the part of the client. This resistance can stem from a number of sources, and is never easy for the interviewer to deal with. The client may see the interviewer as an authority figure and therefore to be opposed. He may be reticent to discuss certain matters which are sensitive and will use silence as a means of avoiding them. Finally, he may just be very anxious about being interviewed and be tonguetied. Silence on the part of the interviewer can be seen as 'threatening' by the client, but if the silence is accompanied by non-verbal support and encouragement for the client, it will then become less threatening and more 'friendly open space' for him to enter when he feels ready.

Listening

An ability to listen effectively is an essential attribute of any interviewer. There is likely to be little dispute about this statement and yet many interviewers do not listen to their clients as effectively as they should do. There are a number of reasons for this. For instance, interviewers sometimes fail to communicate that they have heard the client's message. This is described as passive listening. In contrast, the active listener is attending to his client by hearing, understanding and responding to him. This represents the active involvement of the interviewer and feeds back to the client the fact that the interviewer is 'with him'. The interviewer needs to communicate this and he will use non-verbal cues such as eye contact, body posture, head nodding as well as sounds such as 'Mm-hm'! These all serve to reinforce the fact that the interviewer is listening carefully to the client, is understanding him, and wants to hear more.

Active listening is not necessarily a part of everyday inter-personal communication, and as such, needs to be learned and practiced by most interviewers. There are a number of problems that impair active listening. Selective attention is one of these, and occurs when the interviewer processes only part of the information he receives and ignores the rest. Generally speaking, it is not possible for the interviewer to take in all the verbal and non-verbal messages issued by the client, so there is usually some element of selective attention. However, this becomes a problem when the interviewer is bored, distracted, over anxious,or tired and thus loses concentration.

Another reason for inefficient listening relates to the interviewer's preoccupation with his own responses and the sort of questions he wants to ask. This is often true of those training to be interviewers. In this instance, interviewers are so anxious about what they are going to say next that they fail to listen carefully enough to their client. Some interviewers fall into the trap of anticipating what their client is going to say and jumping to a hasty conclusion. In some instances, there are interviewers who are much more interested and concerned with what they have to say than with what their clients have to say. They are likely to spend more of the interview talking than listening.

Our ability to listen effectively has also to do with how we perceive people. Those interviewers who have prejudices and tend to see others in terms of stereotypes are not likely to hear much more than they actually want to hear. In many cases, this is a serious handicap to understanding the client and makes it very difficult to establish a relationship with him.

The following are goals in listening that Benjamin (1969) suggests:

1.) How the client thinks and feels about himself; how he perceives himself.

2.) What he thinks and feels about others in his world, especially significant others; what he thinks and feels about people in general.

3.) How he perceives others relating to him, how in his eyes others think and feel about him.

4.) How he perceives the material that he, the interviewer, or both wish to discuss; what he thinks and how he feels about what is involved.

5.) What his aspirations, ambitions and goals are.

6.) What defence mechanism he employs.

7.) What coping mechanisms he uses or may be able to use.

8.) What values he holds, what his philosophy of life is.

This is a wide ranging set of goals and it is not suggested that any interviewer should try and work his way through them mechanically, or attempt to deal with them in one interview. However, they do focus the interviewer's attention on aspects of the client that he needs to pay particular attention to.

Non Verbal Communication

Our awareness of non-verbal communication (NVC) has been heightened recently by popularisers such as Desmond Morris. Academic interest in this field of communication has increased steadily over the last two decades, so that today there is substantial literature on the subject. It is beyond the scope of this chapter to enter into a detailed description of all aspects of NVC but it is necessary to deal with some of the more important aspects as they do have a significant bearing upon the relationship between interviewer and client.

NVC serves a number of functions. Argyle (1975) states that it supports and replaces language, expresses emotions and interpersonal attitudes, sends information about personality, as well as playing an important part in ceremony, ritual and the arts. As there is little dispute about the importance of NVC, it is necessary to look in detail at its main characteristics and, in particular, how these play a part in the interview. It is usual to consider aspects of NVC separately, for example, eye contact, proximity etc., and for research purposes this is clearly sensible, but it is as well to remember that inter-personal communication should always be considered as a whole.

The face, eyes and head.

The face is the main vehicle for communicating emotional states, and as such, comprises a wide variety of stimuli. The mouth, eyebrows, nose and skin all combine to 'give off' information. People sometimes use facial expressions to deceive or hide their real feelings, which may be successful, although they may have less success with other parts of their body, i.e. hands and feet. Certainly there is evidence that facial characterstics and expressions do lead to stereotyping and the interviewer should be aware of his own prejudices in this direction. The eyes are used mostly to pick up information, and the direction and duration of gaze is an important part of NVC. For instance, eye contact is often used to signal the start of an interaction or vice-versa. It is important at this stage to note that the amount of gaze appears to be governed by the sex, status and ethnic origin of the people concerned. Thus, for example, those of women, higher status, and Arabs show more gaze than men, those of lower status, and Europeans. Head nods act as a signal to the speaker to continue talking, although rapid head nodding can demonstrate a desire from the listener to speak. Certainly, head nodding and the head inclined to the side are important cues demonstrating that the interviewer is attending to the client.

Gestures and Posture.

Head and arm movements are a frequent part of NVC, as gestures are often signs with agreed meanings. The meanings may vary, according to the social setting and the culture and, as such, gestures can be difficult to understand. Gestures do seem to be a product of the personality, as well as being dependent on mental state, culture, health and fatigue. Body posture also transmits messages. For instance, leaning forward suggests a liking and friendliness, especially if combined with openness of arms and legs.

Spatial Behaviour

Proximity means the distance between the

interviewer and client and this is usually controlled by the former. The closer the distance signifies the more intimate the relationship. Linked to this is orientation or the angle one person faces another. In the case of an interview, the use of desk and its position in relation to the two participants is often crucial in determining orientation. The interviewer facing the client across a desk suggests a less cooperative, less friendly orientation than a side-by-side seating, for instance. There are often physical constraints upon the interviewer as to how he arranges the interview setting, but there may well be opportunities for him to make some adjustment to it, in order to bring it more into line with the way in which he wants to operate.

We respond to NVC as a result of the social skills we have acquired, which will vary from culture to culture, and between social classes. Interviewing demands a greater sensitivity than is normally required in most social encounters. Consequently a greater awareness of NVC is an essential part of effective interviewing. Having said that,it is not suggested that the interviewers view NV signals in an over self-conscious manner, as this will impede their ability to communicate with their clients.

Information and Advice

Leaving the matter of information and advice until last has been quite deliberate. The traditional model of the vocational guidance interview was built on information collection and advice giving, and inevitably this model still has considerable influence on practice. The Seven Point Plan (Rodger 1971) provided a structure, whereby the interviewer collected information under seven headings to build up a profile of the client, and he then used this to advise him on the sorts of occupations that were appropriate. The interviews that Reddy and Brannigan (1982) analysed tended to reflect this model (23% of responses from the interviewer requested information, 15% gave information and 13% gave advice; a total of 51%).

Questioning, and the requesting of information has been dealt with earlier, so no more need be sad specifically about this. However, the place of information, given and received, within the interview, is crucial. How and when information is given needs to be considered carefully. The interview can be a very effective means of transmitting information but to do this, the following criteria needs to be applied. The client should clearly see the information as relevant to him, and it should be expressed in terms appropriate to his level of comprehension. The interviewer should check on how much the client knows already, so that there is no duplication. Finally, the interviewer should check that the client has understood. A long monologue, by the interviewer, should be avoided, as the client is unlikely to remember everything and will also "switch off", after a while. The adoption of a written summary at the end of the interview has been an acknowledgement of the need, for both interviewer and client to recall the substance of the interview.

The step from giving information to giving advice is a short one and not always recognised as such. The interviewer, in selecting to give certain information, is of course making a decision as to what the client needs, and does not need to hear. Benjamin (1969) feels

> "certain that when the interviewer is asked for advice, it is essential that he first of all enables the interviewee to identify and delimit the areas in which he seeks advice. The interviewee should be encouraged to verbalise his hopes and fears, regarding these areas - in brief, to throw as much light as possible on his own situation".

He goes on to say that

> "it is essential that the interviewer ask himself whether he has a need to give advice, in specific instances or generally. Such a need may interfere with the interviewee's struggle to decide what is best for him. The interviewer's need to advise may prematurely cut off the joint examination of the matter under discussion".

Finally, Benjamin makes the important point

> "that the interviewer examines to what extent the interviewee feels he cannot decide alone.

> The interviewee may have learned to regard himself as someone who requires the advice of others, who is incompetent to choose, who must always be dependent on a 'specialist'".

An emphasis on information collection and advice-giving may well fit in with both the interviewer's and the client's expectation of the interview. However, this form of interview may not achieve as much of long term value, as an interview which begins to make the client think for himself, and encourages him to seek information for himself from a variety of sources. Relatively little can actually be 'solved' within the limits of one vocational guidance interview, but a great deal can be initiated. The place of information giving needs to be seen within the wider context of careers education rather than merely the interview, and this will be examined again, in a later chapter.

Some concluding comments.

The interview has been dismissed by writers such as Kline (1975) as 'unreliable, hence invalid'. Their arguments normally centre around their lack of effectiveness, as forms of assessment. Kline certainly sees the assessment of the individual as the point of the guidance interview. This accords with the 'talent matching' guidance interview procedure, but not with more non-directive interviews, where the emphasis is upon the client gaining more insight into himself, in relation to work. Indeed, it could be said that vocational counselling is not concerned with assessment at all, and thus the basis of Kline's criticism disappears.

The whole question of assessing the interview as a guidance instrument is beset with difficulty, and this is certainly one reason why relatively little work has been carried out in this field. Two of the most recent studies (Thomas and Wetherall (1974) and Reddy and Brannigan (1982)) show a fairly high level of satisfaction expressed by the clients. Another study, carried out by two careers officers, in South Tyneside (F. Lloyd and W. Wilson 1980) surveyed all the pupils interviewed in four schools. Nearly 3/4 of the 518 pupils replied, and very high levels of satisfaction were expressed in response to a variety of questions.

Another study of 250 school leavers showed that 72% had found the Careers Officer helpful (Youth Aid 1979). The response of clients is only one measure of effectivness, but it is an important criteria. Reddy and Brannigan also questioned the careers officers about the effectiveness of their interviews, and it was interesting to note that they were a good deal less satisfied than their clients. Perhaps this is because the interviewer and the client had different expectations of the interview, and thus assessed its effectiveness differently.

The question of expectations arose in the large study conducted by Thomas and Wetherall (1974). They found that the students had low standards and expectations as far as careers guidance was concerned, but when asked about the perceived helpfulness of the Careers Officer, 53% responded by saying that he/she had been helpful or very helpful, and only 17% said he/she had been no help at all. Another issue arising from vocational guidance interviews is how clients feel about their usefulness with the benefit of hindsight. One recent survey by M. West and P. Newton (1982) followed up a group of school leavers two and a half years into their working life. When asked about their vocational guidance interview whilst still at school, nearly 80% said that it had been useful; the unfavourable comments mostly came from either those who were very definite about their future or those who had no ideas at all. After two and a half years, 37.5% said they had been helped by their interview in finding a job, 35.2% said that it had made no difference, or had been unhelpful; the remainder had not used the Careers Service to find a job. Bearing in mind that the sample was halved, in size, during the intervening two and a half years, the response can be seen as quite favourable to the Careers Service. This is certainly true if this is compared to the student's assessment of the helpfulness of the school, in terms of careers advice.

The Careers Service branch carried out an interesting study of vocational guidance interviews (D.of E. 1982). This focused on the progress made by the client, in the course of the interview. A framework for analysis was used that looked at:

1.) How far the students narrowed down options.

2.) How well informed the students were about career options.

3.) How realistic the students were in relation to their abilities and the constraints of the labour market.

4.) How aware the students were of options available.

5.) The extent that students had worked out the practical steps necessary to achieve their career objectives.

The sample numbered 680 students, mostly 5th formers, in 196 schools with 204 careers officers, conducting the interviews. The range of ability of the students was wide and the sample was regarded as representative. Careers Service inspectors rated students by means of the five point framework before their interviews. They found that half the students knew what they wanted to do, but even so "the students' need for help in preparing themselves for the transition from school to working life is clearly demonstrated".

The findings of the study are quoted below

1.)Few students show a complete change in orientation of their intentions during the interview.

2.)When change occurs, it is usually in the direction of narrowing down options.

3.)The information needs of 60% of students were met, but for the remainder, some information needs were insufficient. The interview may not be the most appropriate place to meet students' information needs.

4.)By the end of the interview 70% of students had a wider awareness of the range of possible options. About 10% ended their interview with no awareness of the options open to them. It is difficult to see how this group could be offered vocational guidance.

5.)Progress in planning the next practical steps were made by a substantial proportion of students.

6.)Interviews were generally more effective with more vocationally aware students. Different strategies may be more appropriate for the less vocationally aware.

7.)More progress was made where there was a careers education programme and interviews were more efective where careers offices participated in its planning. Greater involvement of careers officers in the school contributed to the effectiveness of the interviews.

8.)Less progress is made when parents are present.

The study indicates that the vocational guidance interview has a useful part to play in a variety of ways. A number of the studies' findings are worth looking at more closely. The overall provision of information at the interview was found to be only partly met and the study concludes that "the interview as a method is particularly ill-suited to both information giving, because so much of it is forgotten by the student and careers education, because of the magnitude of the task". This is linked to the provision of careers education by the schools, and in 29% of the schools there was either no careers education, or it was only provided to some students. It is likely that Careers Officers were trying to compensate for this omission in some of their interviews.

The importance of the careers officers involvement in the schools' careers work, in general, is clear. The regular prescence of the careers officer , in school, and the operation of a 'clinic'system seems to play a significant part in making the interview more effective. Having said this, the study does call for the increased use of screening devices to ascertain who will benefit most from an inteview, and the greater use of group work for such activities as planning.

Setting realistic objectives for the interview is clearly important for both interviewer and client. The following objectives can be seen as realisable in the time normally available, and with the limited preparation by the client that is usual.

- Try to establish a relationship with the client which will encourage him to contact the interviewer again, if the client feels that it is necessary. To achieve this, the interviewer is likely to need to create an 'open space' for the client fo use, rather than subject him to yet another 'lesson'. He also needs to treat each client as an individual.

- Discuss the client's occupational ideas, whatever they are, treating them all seriously. This should be followed by an expansion and development of these ideas with the objective of broadening his horizons.

- Be prepared to give the client information either when he requests it, or when he seems to need it, but at the same time, resisting the temptation to turn the interview into an information dispensing session. It is a better use of the limited time available to refer the client to the relevant sources of information.

- Encourage the client to think more deeply about his values, needs and aspirations related to work. This should really go beyond work to examine the consequences of unemployment.

To do all this satisfactorily may well be impossible in one interview. Limited resources of all kinds can make the practice of vocational guidance very frustrating for practitioners, but perhaps the objectives originally set for those working in this field have been unrealistically high. Ways of using all the resources of the community in vocational guidance will be explored later in the book and suggest a way forward in a particularly difficult time.

Chapter Five

COUNSELLING "In counselling we are concerned with experience. Information and data have little value and relevance in themselves; it is how they are perceived and experienced by the individual himself that proves significant." Peter C. Morea(1972).

Counselling

In recent years, Counselling has made an impact on most of the "Helping Professions" and vocational guidance is no exception. The roots of this chapter are to be found in client centred counselling, and in the work of Carl Rogers in particular. However, there are many other schools of counselling and some of these have a contribution to make in the practice of vocational guidance. John Crites produced a very useful summary of the major approaches to Career Counselling and this will be used as a basis for an examination of the contribution made by Counselling theory. He makes the point that a variety of approaches are needed to deal with the variety of clients and situations which confront the vocational counsellor. In considering these different approaches, Crites examines the model wherein they work and the methods that they use. The models begin with "the diagnosis of the client's problem, proceeding through the process of client-counsellor interviews and culminating in certain outcomes." The methods cover interview techniques, test interpretation and the use of occupational information.

Trait and factor counselling

This constitutes the oldest established and most widely used approach to vocational guidance. Diagnosis lies at the heart of this approach as has been defined by Williamson as

"a process in logical thinking or the 'teasing

> out' from a mass of relevant and irrelevant facts, of a consistent pattern of meaning and an understanding of the client's assets and liabilities together with a prognosis or judgement of the significance of this pattern for future adjustments to be made by the client."

Therefore, the counsellor begins by analysing the client, collecting data about him from a number of sources. This data is then synthesised in some sort of profile, and arising from this, a comparison is made with profiles the counsellor has available of educational and occupational requirements in a wide variety of fields. At this point the client becomes actively involved in considering the prognosis. In other words, the likely implications of his profile are considered and then decisions are made as to the necessary action to be taken by the client. As can be seen, a good deal of the process is carried out by the counsellor and the client is cast in a secondary, relatively reactive role.

The approach is highly rational and action orientated, but it should not mean that the counsellor overlooks the feelings of the client or becomes too judgemental in his attitude. The interview will be essentially pragmatic, giving the counsellor an opportunity to collect data from the client. In a second interview when the data has been profiled, he will discuss the prognosis with the client and agree on the best outcome. Tests and questionnaires form an important part of the diagnosis. The counsellor will use this data to explain, advise and if necessary, persuade the client on various aspects of his occupational choice. He will also use occupational information to support his prognosis, to motivate his client and to readjust him to some occupational choice in some instances.

Trait and factor vocational counselling has come in for a good deal of criticism. This has been based on a number of points. For example, the client can become too dependent on the counsellor and may not carry through the agreed action. In addition, the client does not absorb the mass of test information, and fails to make decisions for himself. It has also been said that the process fails to deal with many of the client's feelings as it is largely a rational and cognitive exercise.

Finally, it is heavily dependent on occupational profiles which are difficult to validate and update.

Client centred vocational counselling

This approach stems only indirectly from the work of Carl Rogers, because he has always been more concerned with the broader psychological adjustment of the client. Diagnosis in the interview is seen as an indication that the counsellor has taken over the responsibility forthe client's problems, and, as such, it is to be avoided. Crites suggests that the goal in client centred therapy is the reorganization of the self, but that in vocational counselling, a more limited goal is appropriate, that of clarifying and implementing the self-concept in an occupational role.

The client centred interview should be displaying three attitudes towards the client. Firstly, congruence, by which is meant genuineness and openness, and a willingness to express feelings. Secondly, understanding and empathy; a sensing of the client's inner world. Finally, acceptance of the client's good and bad points. In recent years, client centred counsellors have become more "active" in their interviewing. By "active" is meant more leading by the counsellor. This trend can be seen as appropriate to the particular needs of vocational guidance.

Tests and questionnaires certainly have a much less prominent place than in trait and factor counselling. Patterson argues that "the essential basis for the use of tests.......is that they provide information which the client needs and wants, information concerning questions raised in counselling". Thus tests and questionnaires are introduced, as requested by the client, and the counsellor reports the results to the client in as objective and non-judgemental a way as possible. The same criteria applies to the use of occupational information. Patterson adds the following:

1.) "The most objective way to provide occupational information and a way which maximizes client initiative and responsibility is to encourage the client to obtain the information from original sources, that is,

> publications, employers and persons in occupations."
>
> 2.) "The client's attitudes and feelings about occupations and jobs must be allowed expression and dealt with therapeutically".

This last criteria is important as the counsellor needs to accept that occupational information has personal meaning to the client and this should be explored within the context of his values as well as what is seen as "objective reality".

Client centred vocational counselling has been criticised as being too passive and, in particular, inappropriate for use with clients who are less articulate, and less able. The constraints of limited time available has also been levelled at this type of counselling, although this comment could be applied to any type of counselling. Certainly there are potential conflicts inherent in the client centred approach and the use of tests, questionnaires and occupational information which are difficult to resolve. However, an awareness of these conflicts and a willingness to treat each client as an individual and thus be flexible, can go a long way to achieving success.

Psychodynamic Vocational Counselling

Only brief reference to psychodynamic vocational counselling will be made, as it is broadly accepted that this approach has less likely application than other counselling approaches. Bordin has been responsible for generating interest in this approach to the vocational. He asserts

> "that insofar as he has freedom of choice, an individual tends to gravitate towards those occupations whose activities permit him to express his preferred ways of seeking gratification and of protecting himself from anxiety.......Psychoanalytic theory suggests that a developmental approach to vocation should examine the full sweep of influences shaping personality from birth, even from conception".

Bordin sees the vocational counselling interview as first seeking to clarify the client's position by means of questions and simplified restatements, and then by use of comparisons, arising from the client's relationships with his family, in particular, explore his difficulties in making vocational decisions. Tests do have their place, but are chosen by the client and the results of these tests should be communicated verbally to the client. The main criticism of the psychoanalytic approach lies in its emphasis on the client's 'internal' factors and the minimization of the 'external' factors. However, Crites does see this approach offering a more individual and flexible orientation than say, trait and factor counselling.

Developmental Career Counselling

Donald Super is the main 'architect' of this approach. He outlined three areas of appraisal, which provide a working basis for the counsellor. Problem appraisal considers the client's vocational thinking in terms of, for example, his ability to make decisions, his family's involvement in his choice, his maturity and his perception of occupations. Personal appraisal is concerned with a psychological 'picture' of the client based upon data from various sources, e.g. tests, interview, school. Prognostic appraisal deals with predictions about the client's future behaviour in relation to the counsellor, and later in a job. In summary, Super stated that

> "the assumption underlying this approach is that one way to understand what an individual will do in the future is to understand what he did in the past. It postulates that one way to understand what he did in the past is to analyse the sequences of events and the development of characteristics in order to ascertain the recurring themes and underlying trends".

At all stages, the client is actively involved in the appraisal process and the objective is a cooperative but realistic outcome. Central to this approach is the career life stage of the client, for this will determine the sort of approach to be adopted by the counsellor. Thus, with younger, more career immature clients, the counsellor will be less concerned with choice, but more concerned with developing his readiness for choice. Super's basic premise is that people are both rational and emotional, and therefore vocational counselling should build upon both elements. This is illustrated by such questions as "What sort of person do I think I am?" and "What sort of person would I like to be?"

The interview should follow the following cycle:

1.) Non directive problem exploration and self concept portrayal.

2.) Directive topic setting for further exploration.

3.) Non directive reflection and clarification of feeling for self acceptance and insight.

4.) Directive exploration of factual data from tests, occupational pamphlets, extra curricular experiences, etc., for reality testing.

5.) Non directive exploration and working through of attitudes and feelings aroused by reality testing.

6.) Non directive consideration of possible lines of action for help in decision making.

Tests have their place in developmental career counselling but only when administered in a discriminating way and when the client has been involved in every stage of the process. The most appropriate occupational information is that which deals with the description of career patterns in different occupational pursuits. This sort of information has not been available in many cases, and the counsellor may have to build up a selection of this information on his own initiative.

Developmental career counselling is seen by Crites as the "most comprehensive and coherent system of assisting clients with career problems which has as yet been formulated".

Behavioural Career Counselling

Anxiety reduction and decision making are the two main foci of this type of counselling. Lack of information about self and work, due to a limitation of experience, leads to indecision and sometimes to anxiety. This state is not infrequently attributed to domineering or over demanding parents.

This type of counselling is based upon learning theory principles, and as such has a number of techniques to offer. The idea of positive reinforcement could be used with clients, whereby they are rewarded for carrying out certain tasks related to occupational choice. Likewise, social modelling can be applied to clients. In this case, some aspect of desired behaviour, e.g. effective job interview performance, is demonstrated, on film, tape or in practice, and the client or client's behaviour is progressively modified towards the model. An interesting example of this is quoted by Ross(1981). He used hypnotic imagery with a group of undergraduates, by presenting seven role profiles to them. These role profiles described the typical activities of certain graduate occupations. The experience seemed to clarify the students' minds, and encouraged them to apply for specific jobs.

Systematic desensitisation techniques have been used successfully in the treatment of phobias, and have also been applied to anxiety reduction for those who have particular difficulty in employment interviews. Assertive practice techniques can also be applied in the same way. By means of role plays, the client can learn to realise his potential much more freely.

Extended role play situations and simulation exercises can be seen as following behavioural principles. These opportunities have been limited to small groups of sixth formers and undergraduates, on the whole, but seem to offer encouraging results. Behavioural counselling has been criticised for manipulating the client. This is countered by the behaviourists who say that they focus on what actually concerns the client, i.e. some aspect of behaviour, rather than looking more widely and diffusely at him, and that this is ultimately more helpful and effective.

A Problem Solving Approach

The work of Gerard Egan has been influential in the United States for some years, and has aroused interest in the U.K. as well. In a recent paper

(Egan 1982), he suggests a framework for helping with Four stages outlined. The counsellor is seen as a consultant who is necessary as most people do not approach problems systematically and thoroughly.

Stage One - Clarification

The consellor needs to communicate empathy, listen actively and probe. He is attempting to help his client assess the problem, and then focus upon it and explore it further.

Stage Two - Managing the problem

The counsellor will need to help the client challenge himself, and possibly, to challenge the client directly. It may be necessary for the client to develop a new perspective on themselves. At this point, the problem(s) should be clearly defined and the counsellor needs to move on to problem handling by means of arriving at workable goals. These goals have to be clear, measurable, realistic, based on achievements, in keeping with the values of the client and within a reasonable time frame. Goal setting is the central point of the process.

Stage Three - Dealing with the goals

The counsellor can help the client explore as many different ways of achieving the goals as possible. This will allow for the client trying a number of different strategies, in order to succeed. Counsellor and client should draw up an 'action contract' which will set out the client's tasks, and provide a stimulus for activity.

Stage 4 - Implementation and evaluation

The counsellor cannot carry out the 'action contract' but he can help by pre-viewing or simulating certain situations, e.g. role-playing in interviews. Evaluation of the 'action plan' is best done on an on-going basis, so as to help with any necessary adjustments.

Much of this will be familiar to those working in vocational guidance already. It seems to establish a sense of order in the mind of the client, by working through a series of tasks. Egan (1982), maintains that "in all effective helping, no matter what model or school of helping is being used, the goals of all these tasks are achieved either by clients on their own or in collaboration with the helper". He goes on to say "the logic of the problem solving seems to be embedded in our brains and bones, but somehow this logic does not always make its way into our behaviour". It is up to the helper to initiate this inherent problem solving capacity that we all possess.

Fantasy in vocational counselling

This is an activity that has interested vocational counsellors in the United States in recent years, and has been the subject of research within its broader uses in psychotherapy, (J.I. Morgan and T.M. Skovholt, 1977). There is a problem of credibility as far as fantasy is concerned, as it is often seen as frivolous or as a manifestation of maladjustment. Daydreaming, a sort of fantasising, has been studied and has found to be widely practiced, while some of this research indicates that there is a 90 minute ongoing daytime cycle of daydreaming. It is interesting to note that Ginzberg (1972) has revised his original theory as regards fantasy. He no longer limits it to young people, but feels it can have usefulness in later life. Holland and Gottfredson (1975), maintain, arising from research based on large sample, that "the findings imply that a person's occupational daydreams have considerable psychological meaning; a pattern of related aspirations implies decision making ability, psychological integration and predictability". There is certainly enough evidence to support the view that fantasy and daydreaming is an important area of our experience, and as such, warrants the attention of the vocational counsellor.

Two sorts of fantasies can be used by counsellors. Spontaneous fantasies can be used in the same way that any other information is used, and can be gathered by merely asking the client about his occupational daydreams. Guided fantasy involves three stages.

Firstly, clients need to be relaxed and receptive. This requires them to be sitting comfortably or lying on the floor. Relaxation exercises involving muscle tensing and relaxing, deep breathing and imagery can all be used.

Secondly, clients are asked to let their imaginations take over, and then the counsellor asks them to imagine a typical working day, perhaps five years hence. He takes them through the day. Some examples from Skovholt and Hoenniger (1974) serve to illustrate the sort of script the counsellor might use:

> "Let your imagination take you five years into your future as I talk, just let any images come that will. Don't answer my questions aloud. Just let the images form (pause). You are just awakening from a good night's sleep. You lie in bed, just a minute longer, before getting up and doing the things you usually do before breakfast, (pause)".

The counsellor will continue in this vein, following a typical working day through to bed time, pausing regularly to allow the client's imagination to work fully. It is also important to phrase questions in an open way to allow clients to let their imagination work as freely as possible. Clearly using fantasy makes certain demands on the counsellor, who needs to feel confident in its use, if it is to be used effectively.

Thirdly, fantasies have to be processed, and the counsellor needs to help his clients to do this. Doing this in a group is considered best, as the discussion arising from a variety of fantasies can be very rewarding. Clients enjoy guided fantasy, and they can disclose as much as they choose in discussion. Sharing in a group is rewarding, and fantasy exploration does bring out material that might not normally arise in an interview. The main area of difficulty tends to centre around the mechanics of the technique, e.g. the relaxation exercises, voice quality, pacing, etc.

The place of counselling in vocational guidance

There is probably still some confusion about the place of counselling in vocational guidance. This was certainly true in 1975, when Ruth Lancashire investigated practitioners opinions. She found that most practitioners saw counselling as "an umbrella term of which vocational counselling was an example". In her concluding comments, she saw vocational advisers as information officers, organisers and educators,

> "but we become counsellors when we sit down with our clients and help them to work through the role work is likely to take in their lives, what they are likely to be able to contribute and the satisfactions for which they are looking, and what this all adds up to in general and specific vocational terms".

Counselling is often described in terms of skills and is helpful to identify these skills under certain headings, and in some order of sequence.

1.)Listening - attending to the client by noting verbal and non verbal behaviour. Paraphrasing the client's basic messages. Clarifying the client's statements, and checking the accuracy of hearing.

2.)Reflecting - responding to feelings and experiences. Repeating the client's ideas in new words.

3.)Leading - encouraging discussion, focussing to try and avoid confusion. Open questioning.

4.)Summarising - pulling themes together.

5.)Confronting - feeding back opinions, honestly to help the client. Describing and sharing feelings.

6.)Interpreting - using questions to enable awareness, use of symbols and imagery.

7.)Informing - giving information and making suggestions.

Counselling and guidance in fact represent a continuum of counselling skills, which is clearly demonstrated in figure 5.1.

Figure 5.1

A spectrum of face to face consultancy skills
(From Watts, Super and Kidd - "Career Development in Britain")

Interpretation and diagnosis

Behavioural Reinforcement

Training and Development activity

Suggestion for next action

Giving Information

Reflection of feeling

Confrontation

'Open' Questioning

Reflection of content

Summarisation

Clarification

←——————————————————————→

Counsellor as expert and/or client as passive | Counsellor as facilitator and/or client active

Watts et al described skilled counsellors as being capable of occupying all positions on this continuum depending on the needs of their clients. Certainly, these needs vary amongst clients and also within the same client, over a period of time. Counselling training adds another dimension to the work of those in vocational guidance, by enabling them to operate in a wider range of ways, and, at a deeper level.

It is worth exploring the dynamics of the counselling interview, in order to better understand its nature. Nelson Jones(1982) has expressed this diagrammatically in figure 5.2.

As the counselling relationship develops, the client should become increasingly aware of his thoughts and feelings, develop a greater self acceptance, and by trusting the counsellor, feel safer about self disclosure. Equally, his private thoughts, feelings and expectations are likely to become more public to the counsellor as the interview(s) progress. The right hand column highlights the fact that the counsellor is also experiencing the interview, is part of the counselling process, and cannot be a detached, 'scientific' observer. He needs to deal with his own thoughts and feelings, as well as his client's.

Figure 5.2

Diagrammatic representation of the counselling interview (from Nelson Jones, 1982)

Client Private	Client and Counsellor Public	Counsellor Private
Private thoughts, feelings and expectations	Clients verbal communications and self exploration Counsellors verbal communication	Private thoughts, feelings and expectations
Availability to awareness of thoughts and feelings	Clients intended and unintended bodily communication	Availability to awareness of thoughts and feelings
Degree of self-acceptance	Counsellors intended and unintended bodily communication	Degree of self-acceptance
Anticipation of risk in self-disclosures	Accuracy of clients perceptions of counsellors communications	Internal dialogue
Internal dialogue	Accuracy of counsellors perceptions of clients communications	

COUNSELLING

Counsellors need to examine their attitudes, and feelings, towards their clients. Fitzgerald and Crites (1980) draws attention to a good deal of evidence of sexism practiced by counsellors, in the United States. This is reflected in negative views expressed about women entering non-traditional occupations, and an endorsement of the view that women are primarily homemakers. These sorts of views are likely to be common amongst some of those working in vocational guidance in this country. Quite clearly, careers officers and counsellors cannot avoid introducing their own values into their work with clients, so it is imperative that they recognise this and examine how far these values might be affecting these relationships, and influencing their client's choices. Barry and Wolf (1962) maintain that those in counselling are generally "staunch upholders of middle-class values", and accordingly will uphold the worth of education and work, possibly distancing themselves from some of their clients.

Likewise, they state that

> "traditional vocational guidance has operated on the assumption that everyone's values are the same, that everyone is ambitious and eager to get ahead, that everyone considers work of equal importance".

These assumptions are likely to be incorrect for some clients, and counsellors, careers officers and teachers should be sensitive to this.

It is true to say that the counselling function has not become fully established as an integral part of vocational guidance practice in this country, unlike the United States. Keele University Counselling Service is one notable exception, with vocational, personal and educational counselling, all being offered by the same staff. Newsome, Thorne and Wyld (1975) have described vocational counselling as

> "not merely concerned with the provision of information, nor even with the exploration of aptitudes and interests. It is concerned rather with the whole person, as he seeks to come to an understanding of himself, his values and his aims".

Despite this forthright statement, Counselling

services in higher and further education have been developed separately from Careers Advisory Services, although, in some cases, they have worked closely together.

Summary

There is a good deal of ambivalence about the place of counselling in vocational guidance, and some of this arises both from a lack of understanding of counselling, and a certain mystification that has grown up around counselling. Hopson and Scally (1979) describe counselling as "only one form of helping. It is decidedly not the answer to all human difficulties, though it can be extremely productive for some people, sometimes". However, Hopson (1982) adds "there is a need for the particular interpersonal skills categorised as counselling skills to be understood and used by people at large, but particularly by all people, who have the welfare of others as part of their occupational roles".

One of the central issues of counselling is the question of its 'political' dimension. Carl Rogers (1978) has acknowledged that the approach to counselling, that he has pioneered, invites the client to become aware and take more control of his life. Individual change inevitably raises the question of institutional change. Lewis and Lewis(1977) describe a counsellor's work as bringing them face to face with poverty, racism, sexism and all sorts of institutions that stifle individualism. Those working in vocational guidance are often faced with these issues, especially the problem of unemployment. How they choose to deal with these issues has important consequences, not just for their clients, but for themselves as well.

Chapter Six

CAREERS EDUCATION

"Careers Education is not a new concept; it identifes and accentuates certain specific features on the profile of education familiar to every secondary school teacher" DES Survey 18(1973)

As earlier chapters have indicated, education has always been one of the key socialsing agents in society and, as such, has inevitably 'prepared' youngsters for entry to employment. Although formal careers education is a relatively new part of the curriculum, schools have had an important role in teaching pupils to "know their place" in the occupational structure. The curriculum under the tripartite system (which has never been fully superceded by comprehensivisation and may well be revived in the near future) was designed to prepare pupils, from eleven, for the professions, for higher level technical occupations, and for craft, semi-skilled or unskilled jobs. Careers Education programmes emerged with the growth of comprehensive schools, and it is these formal arrangements that will be examined in this chapter.

Writers have seen the school's part in socialization into work in two distinctly different ways (Ryrie 1977). There are those who see the school as failing to provide a smooth transition to work. Bazalgette (1978) is critical of schools for not provding the sort of relationships with adults which could help them to take their place in the adult world. He feels that schools emphasise academic work and encourage dependency, rather than encourage young people to develop autonomy. Scharff (1976) perceives school as a sort of 'womb' from which it is painful to emerge, whilst White and Brockington (1978) see school as rejecting, and being rejected, by a significant minority, who thus fail to gain much, if any help, in making the transition.

The other group of writers are critical of schools as being too well integrated into the outside world. Ashton and Field (1976) see schools dividing pupils into three broad bands, which coincide with the three broad occupational groupings. Willis (1977) also sees schools in these terms. He describes how a group of working class 'lads' reject the school culture which represent the "relations of domination in society as a whole". The fact that these 'lads' enter manual, dead end jobs as a result of their rejection of school values is functional to the economy, as their labour is required. In a sense, the school is helping to produce the necessary labour force for the economy. Both perspectives, although seemingly totally opposed, can be seen as accurately describing the school's relationship to the economy and working opportunities. The school's role, and that of careers education, in relation to a depressed economy, and unemployment, will be examined more closely, later in this chapter.

Objectives

In 1973 the D.E.S. produced "Careers Education in Secondary Schools" which set out three objectives:

1.)To help boys and girls to achieve an understanding of themselves, and to be realistic about their strengths and weaknesses.

2.)To extend the range of their thinking about opportunities in work, and in life generally.

3.)To prepare them to make considered choices.

These three statements may strike the reader as unexceptional, and requiring little comment. However, if they are examined more closely, it will be seen that they do contain some very important assumptions. Firstly, there is an emphasis or self-understanding, which implies an explanation of values, feelings and attitudes, as well as interests and abilities. The latter are more conventional areas of individual development that education has been concerned with, whilst the former have been treated with a good deal of caution by education. Secondly, the notion of "extending the range of their thinking about opportunities in work" suggests a move away from narrowing of opportunities that selection at eleven plus divined, towards a less determinist view of pupils' life chances. It is worth adding that girls as well as boys are mentioned, so again there is an underlying implication that the restricted range of work, that girls might enter, might be widened. "Life generally" is also referred to, when extended thinking is mentioned, and this puts careers education firmly into the broader context of social education. This can be seen as a success for those who had been actively promoting the view that vocational guidance is an integral part of educational and personal development, within schools (Daws 1972).

When considering careers education, it is necessary to ask "why" before examining "what", "how", and "when". When attempting to answer "why", the sort of answer produced will depend on the standpoint of the questioner. The employer, the teacher, the pupil, and the parents may well express different opinions of careers education. Certainly, there has always been a strongly expressed view that schools need to be more 'relevant' places, and that careers education can and ought to play a vital part in this. Employers, in particular, have subscribed to this opinion. Another reason, expressing a rather different view, is that of giving the pupil more control over his life, by equipping him to make better choices in general. Ultimately, of course, the question of "whose interests does careers education serve?" ought to be asked.

Barry and Wolf (1962) outlined six principles for a school guidance programme which, to some extent, answer this question.

1.) The programme should serve the pupil, not the teacher or the school.

2.) It should start with a holistic approach to the individual. This is a call for integrating careers education into the mainstream of personal development carried out by the school.

3.) The programme must broaden the interests, experiences, learnings and aspirations of the pupils. This is very challenging, as it means pupils need not just to learn passively, but be active and have the chance to experience and really broaden their self-knowledge, and knowledge of the working world.

4.) The programme should be judged by how well it meets the pupil's needs. Thus evaluation, based on consumer opinion, is necessary.

5.) What is done for one need not be done for all. This is not a plea for the academically able to be excused careers education! It is a reminder that pupils' needs vary and, as far as possible, careers education should cater for this

6.) The programme must be professional. This means careers teachers require training and sufficient resources plus encouragement, in order to do their work properly.

In discussion of common problems in careers education in Britain and the United States, Watts and Herr (1976) identify four particular approaches which focus on underlying socio-political aims. Social control is the first approach, and this applies to careers education that is concerned with adapting individuals to jobs 'realistically' open to them. Roberts (1977) would justify careers education on these grounds, and in sociolgical terms, it could be described as functional. It is functional to the occupational structure in that 'suitable' people were being encouraged to fill the jobs available and functional to individuals in that they were saved the frustration of 'aiming too high'.

Careers education can be seen as an agent of social change. Watts and Herr describe it as "basically Marxist". This is true in so far as the Marxist critique of the capitalist system is probably the leading intellectual advocacy of social change, but it would be misleading to suggest that this is the only basis for this approach. For example, the Ecology party document (1981) on the future of work advocates radical social change, and could be included in careers education, but it is not Marxist.

The third approach that concentrates upon individual change has connections with the second approach in that it is critical of the allocation of occupational opportunities, but different in the sense that it does not imply wholesale changes in the nature of the economy. The emphasis is upon encouraging pupils whose aspirations are lower than they might be, for instance black pupils, girls, and pupils from working class families. This implies an intervention by the school to alter the 'status quo', and could be accused of being 'unrealistic', as well as potentially harmful to these pupils it purports to be helping. Roberts (1977) has argued that such an approach does not recognize the powerful constraints of opportunity-structure, and rather than create change, leads to individual frustration.

The fourth approach is non-directive. It aims to make pupils aware of the full range of opportunities as well as "helping them to be more autonomous in choosing the alternative suited to their needs and preferences". It recognizes that pupils will have different values and may decide to respond differently to work, but does not seek to influence these decisions. These four different approaches illustrate the range of underlying objectives of careers educations programmes. The first approach is the traditional objective and still well represented, whilst the fourth gained ground with the growth in interest in non-directive counselling. The second approach is unlikely to be in evidence to any extent, whilst the third is likely to be found where some particularly committed teacher or school has decided to confront the issue of sexism or racism.

Law (1981) suggests other ways of looking at Careers Education. It can be seen as a cosmetic. This is where careers education is not permitted to interfere with the existing curriculum, but is still officially given prominence. Little real effort is made to use careers education creatively, it is done without any real committment. Law describes validation of the school's "success" as being another way of using careers education. Here the emphasis will be on developing links with employers, so as to maximise the chance of the school's pupils getting jobs. This may be done to increase the prestige of the school rather than enable pupils to get the jobs best suited to them.

These two approaches do not involve any real changes in curriculum priorities, neither does the third, where careers education is a supplement. In this case, the school provides a resources centre, typically a careers room or an area of the library with careers materials for the individual to consult at lunchtime, break, or after school. Some interviews and group work will be carried out. Careers education becomes a "real" subject when it appears regularly on the timetable. Once this has happened an evolution often takes place. The programme begins by offering presentations by employers, and a general focus on occupations and self assessement. In time, this can develop into a more varied and challenging programme involving more 'participative' activities. These activities are typified by the Schools Council Careers Education and Guidance project materials. They call for a wider perception of the topics to be covered and a more innovative way of dealing with them. This different style of teaching, and the challenging nature of the material can put careers education at the 'margin' within the school as a whole.

The actual infusion of careers education into the school curriculum has been achieved by some schools, as Law and Watts (1977) noted in their research project. This can occur in one of two ways. It can come 'bottom up' from less senior staff such as tutors, who initiate activities independently. In time their work becomes 'legitimised' and co-ordinated into a school programme. In other cases, it can be 'top down', with the initiative from the senior staff. In one school that Law and Watts investigated, they found a 'school and community enterprise' approach to Careers Education in operation. This was based on the school's overall ethos which was one of accountability and involvement in the neighbourhood. Locally relevant courses were set up, various members of the community came into the school to take part in its programme, and pupils went out into local industry on carefully prepared schemes. This particular approach will be examined more closely, later in the chapter, as it does present a particularly interesting and challenging way of carrying out careers education.

The Structure and Content of Programmes

There are many different published programmes of careers education and many more 'home grown' programmes operating in individual schools. Curragh and McGleenan (1980) have outlined a set of components for a careers education programme.

1.) Formal component - all classified careers information.

2.) Informal component - Human models, work experience, etc.

3.) Acquisition and categorisation of information about the world of work - structure and organization of the world of work, occupational life styles, opportunities etc.

4.) Development of skills - skills associated with problem solving communication, psychomotor domain, etc.

5.) Development of self concepts and self orientated attitudes - interests, needs, values, various competencies, personality traits etc.

6.) Career decision making strategies - identifying preferences, hypothesis formulation and testing, selecting models, applying strategies etc.

7.) Crystallisation of career choices - becoming committed, accepting responsibility, reality testing etc.

8.) Career actuality - specification, assessing/evaluating a specialisation, final implementation etc.

This set of components focuses on the place of both formal and informal information, the development of process skills and the encouragement of decision making.

Careers education initially focused on 'opportunity awareness', a broadening of the individual's knowledge of what sort of jobs were available, what qualifications were required, what rewards were associated with these jobs. This was a natural focus, as this sort of information was fairly accessible, relatively easy to disseminate, and uncontentious forthe most part. It also provided a preparation for the vocational guidance interview, which was supposed to cater for the assessement of the individual's capabilities and motivation towards particular sorts of jobs. In time, careers education broadened its brief to include 'self awareness' as a necessary part of its programme. This exercise was more difficult to achieve, for various reasons. It is more complex, less definite, and focuses ultimately on individuals. There were additional objectives identified as well; those of "decision making" and "helping prepare for the transition from school to work".

These four broad cases provide a convenient focus for examining a number of well known published programmes of careers education. The intention of this exercise will be to look at common areas, and different learning techniques employed by these programmes. The programmes considered are:

Exercises in Personal and Careers Education - B.Hopson and P.Hough

Life Skills Training Manual - Community Service Volunteers

Life After School - J.McGuire and P. Priestley

Lifeskills teaching programmes No.1, No.2. B.Hopson and M.Scally.

Practical Aspects of Guidance 1 - Careers Education - D.R.Cleaton and R.J.Foster

Work Parts 1,2,3 - Schools Council Careers Education and Guidance Project

Work Shuffle - B.Hopson and M.Scally.

1. Opportunity Awareness

A number of the programmes above are more broadly concerned with personal development than careers education, so it is not surprising that they devote little attention to this particular area. Work 1,2, and 3 provide the majority of material. Three headings emerged from the various relevant exercises; job information, the nature of work, and the job market.

a.) Job Information - examples
    Finding it - sources
    Types of careers literature - looking at

it critically, examining what pupils already know about jobs.

b.) Nature of Work - examples
Job Satisfacton
Job analysis and job description.
Variety of jobs and how they link together.
Working conditions.
Skills required by jobs.

c.) Job Market - examples
Job prospects survey.
Pattern of work locally and nationally.
Consideration of how pupils restrict their own job prospects.

These activities call for a variety of teaching styles. For instance, some are best achieved through individual or group project work. This might involve pupils carrying out surveys in the local community, interviewing adults about their jobs and simulation exercises.

2. Self Awareness

Hopson and Hough (1973) describe self awareness as

> "a degree of consciousness about one's person - body, mind, needs attitudes and values - which most of us could develop more fully than we do..... The value of self awareness then lies not just in the way it can help in making decisions in school, nor only in relation to vocational choice, but as part of a preparation for the whole range of life experiences."

Focus on self knowledge is clearly central to programmes of personal and careers education, so all the programmes under consideration devote attention to this topic. Four broad areas emerge from the various programmes. They deal with self assessment, relating to others, face to face skills and life styles.

a.) Self Assessement - Examples
Self description by writing down personal details or self portrayal by drawing a

self portrait (which is then shared in a group)
Constructing a list of personal priorities, (then comparing it with others).
Peer Interviewing.
Looking at talents (how they are encouraged and discouraged; find out about hidden talents).
How to be positive about oneself.
Exercises to explore the senses and feelings.
The above activities are conducted in pairs or groups and call for the participation of all those involved. They explore a whole range of different aspects of the self and would be used with 3rd or 4th year pupils.

b.) Relating to others - examples.

Exploring boundaries between ourselves and others.
Making relationships.
Expressing trust and depending on others.
Giving and receiving feedback - positive and negative.

c.)Face to Face skills - examples.

Listening to others
Looking at non-verbal communication.
Distinguishing between assertive, aggressive and non-assertive behaviour.

With these activities, role play and the use of video can be very useful at times. With both b.) and c.) exercises can be specifically adapted to relate to work, or selection interviews.

d.) Lifestyles - examples.

Lifelines, sketching your own life story.
Ideal lifestyles
Looking at the kind of future success wanted
Comparison of roles attributed to men and women

There is a developmental emphasis on these activities, in that some look back in time, whilst others project into the future. Fantasy can be an important feature of some exercises.

3. Decision making

This is an activity that link together self awareness and opportunity awareness at various stages of a pupil's career and beyond. Two distinct, but closely linked areas of decision making emerge from the programmes under examination; educational and vocational.

a.) Educational - examples

Subject options at 13+
Leaving at 16 or staying on.

b.) Vocational - examples

Career decisions.

Some programmes lay a lot of emphasis on decision making. This might involve an examination of how they make decisions already, suggesting a strategy, encouraging them to make decisions safely through simulations, role plays and real situations, and then evaluating what they have done.

4. Preparation for Transition

Typically, this occupies time during the fifth year at school when many pupils will be leaving. Four topics come within this area; the selection process, settling in at work, unemployment and coping with change.

a.) The Selection Process - examples.

Interviews
Application
Job search techniques.

b.) Settling in at Work - examples

Punctuality
Relationships at work.
Trade Unions
Tax, Insurance, etc.

c.) Unemployment - examples

Rights and benefits.

Coping with unemployment.
Explanations for unemployment.

d.) Coping with change - examples.

Impact of leaving school on relationships
Future changes in work, role of men and women etc.
Looking back at changes and forward to possible changes

Again, a whole range of teaching methods are appropriate with these activities. For instance, using video for interview practice is becoming more common. Role play can be used; parents, former pupils, employers, trade unionists, etc. can usefully contribute; whilst work experience is also very relevant. Unemployment is now such a major problem that it has altered the role of the Careers Service and is likely to influence the nature of education through M.S.C. initiatives. For this reason, unemployment will be considered separately in a later chapter. However, it does require some further discussion in relation to career education programmes.

Watts (1979) describes seven broad curricular objectives relating to the issue of unemployment. He maintains that schools too often avoid this issue, whereas they have a responsibility to confront it. The treatment of unemployment should be "experience based and action oriented" and should aim to engender self-confidence in pupils. An example of this is giving pupils not just knowledge about their benefits and rights, but also the confidence to claim them. Watts makes the point that too much emphasis on job finding and keeping can "sustain the myth that there are satisfying jobs available for anyone who has the skills and persistence to find them".

The seven objectives are as follows:

a.) Employability skills - equipping pupils with skills to help them find and keep a job. Adaptability awareness - extending the range of possible opportunities that pupils will feel are open to them. These two objectives are, in a sense, an 'insurance' against the possibility of being unemployed.

b.) Survival skills - equipping pupils with the knowledge and skills needed to survive when unemployed.

Contextual awareness - help pupils determine the extent to which the responsibility for being unemployed lies with society, rather than with them.

Leisure skills - equipping pupils to make good use of their increased leisure time.

These three objectives are concerned with coping with unemployment and recognising that it is a condition that is going to effect a large number of youngsters at some stage in their lives.

c.) Alternative opportunity awareness - inform pupils of official alternatives to work and unemployment, i.e. further education, training schemes.

Opportunity creation skills - equipping pupils with the knowledge and skills to be able to create their own employment.

Hopson and Scally (1982) have produced a teaching programme which "helps to broaden the understanding of the nature of work". It provides six exercises, most of which are designed to be used with school leavers, but some could be used with older persons who are either employed or unemployed. This is possible as the programme focuses on work values and aims to maximise people's chances of satisfying them " through the complete panorama of life roles and not simply through the role of the paid employee".

The programme's objectives are really very radical because they dispute the 'conventional wisdom' that only paid employment is work, and that other activities such as D.I.Y. and housekeeping, are not work. Paid employment is also seen as essential to self esteem, personal identity, and status in the community, whilst unpaid activities carry much less 'weight'. Hopson and Scally maintain that this is a false distinction, and that thinking must change to cater for a world which does not have enough paid full-time employment for those who either want it, or who are expected to have it. In conclusion, they state that "it is likely to become possible once again in Post-industrial Society to accrue status from one's work other than merely from that for which one gets paid".

Careers Education and Girls

In 1980, the Schools Council set up a committee to consider the problem of sex bias in education. A year later, a three year Sex differentiation project was started, and is working with teacher groups in several LEAs. Amongst the topics they are considering are careers education and sex differences in career aspiration, confidence and motivation in pupils. These are topics that should certainly concern all those involved in vocational guidance.

Hansen (1974) suggested a number of strategies to consider.

1. Awareness of the counsellor's own attitudes, expectations and practices regarding women clients. It is difficult to be objective about one's own behaviour, and many practices are unconscious in fact. Recording interviews, gaining feedback from colleagues and clients are ways of examining our behaviour.

2. Need to know and help clients obtain accurate information about trends in work and society in general. Many changes in employment patterns, legislation, family structure etc. have occured in recent years, and counsellors must keep up to date with these and be able to transmit them to their clients. 'Breakthrough' (EOC undated) is a visual collection of examples of women doing 'unconventional jobs' and could be used in schools.

3. An awareness of sex bias in careers literature, tests, and questionnaires. The Equal Opportunities Commission (1980) produced a booklet looking at this area and recommended positive action. To quote " Careers teachers and careers officers can positively encourage young people to widen horizons through careers education programmes before the stage of third year options. Part of such programmes could

include a critical examination of sex roles and images of men and women in society. Frequent positive steps need to be taken to increase awareness of work opportunities in non-traditional areas. Careers education has a central role to play in challenging the stereotyped and entrenched attitudes towards men and women".

4. A need to help young men and women become aware of the options available to them - in education, work, life styles and career patterns. The emphasis on men and women is important here as the stereotyping of women effects men as well. Careers education should be a mixed activity with girls being exposed to the same experiences as boys.

5. A need to help boys and girls learn the processes involved in decision making. Here the emphasis is on presenting girls with the view that they have choices regarding their future and that they can make decisions for themselves.

6. Provide girls with a variety of role models with whom they can identify, and from whom they can learn that multiple roles are possible, desirable and real. "Girls into science and technology" is an example of this. This is an E.O.C. sponsored project which uses intervention strategies in order to overcome some of the factors stopping girls from taking up options in physical science and technical crafts. The D.E.S. has also funded a three year research project, Girls in "male" jobs. It considers the emotional and social implications of girls in industry and how they cope with the problems of working in a traditionally male world. The evidence emerging from the project suggests that girls still get ill-informed or biased careers advice.

7. A need to involve parents more systematiclly and developmentally in the career development process of boys and girls. Parents obviously play a crucial role in influencing their children's attitudes, and they should not be ignored.

CRAC produced a booklet "Male and Female - choosing your role in modern society" (1974) which outlined a course that would get pupils to question their own sex sterotypes and look at the options open to them. More recently, McRobbie and McCabe (1981) have written a rather more radical book. This presents feminist perspectives on careers, romance and sexuality, girls' magazines, and the reality of being a black girl in Britain today. It's purpose is broadly consciousness raising rather than providing specific exercises for a careers education programme. It is also encouraging to see a conference on "Non-sexist practice in the Careers Service. Making it Work", being held in 1982. It recommended action in a number of areas - employers, schools, N.T.I. occupational choice theory, careers service, careers literature. Hopefully, some results will stem from this initiative.

In conclusion, it is worth drawing attention to West and Newton's study of school leavers (1983) which found "consistently unfavourable experiences of females leaving school". A high level of alienation from work was reported by the girls in their survey which wa based on their conditions of work which were objectively worse than the boys. They were paid less, had less chance to work overtime, and were less likely to receive formal training. The girls felt much less able to change the situation and fell back on marriage and having children as a means of "fulfilling themselves". As West and Newton point out, "females exchange of dependence on parents, for dependence on a husband, in return for adult status, can create frustration and depression after marriage". They suggest that "it is important for schools to help females consider establishing their social identity in spheres other than marriage".

Occupational Information

Clarke (1980) in reviewing research carried out into occupational information stated that "the picture on average appears to be one of an ill informed somewhat apathetic adolescent who still relies on parental advice for occupational information, which, due to its complex, diverse and dynamic nature, they are ill equipped to supply". Careers education is partly about providing pupils with occupational information, and this statement therefore suggests that it has been failing in part of its task. Kirton's study of sixth form boys (1976) showed that over two-thirds needed more information, and that they wanted more precise details about the jobs content, more about unusual jobs and about the total range available, post 'A' level. Rauta and Hunt's study of fifth form girls showed fewer girls expressing dissatisfaction with the information available to them, although the majority would have liked more visits from employers and colleges.

The range and quality of occupational information has improved considerably in recent years thanks to organizations such as C.O.I.C. and C.R.A.C., and this has gone some way to improving the situation described by studies like Kirton's. An earlier study by Hayes (1971) showed that the psycho-social aspects of work such as contact with people and how one's life style is affected by work were given little attention in careers literature in comparison with the economic aspects of work like pay, and entry requirements. However, when a group of apprentices were asked about what was important to them once at work, the psycho-social aspects assumed much greater importance than had been originally imagined. Hayes stated that this sort of information had been largely neglected by those working in vocational guidance, because it was not readily available and it was felt to lack objectivity. Making such information available is not enough however, it needs to be processed in such a way that clients will have an opportunity to assimilate it properly. This requires both time and staff sufficiently committed and trained to accomplish this demanding task.

A number of more recent developments in the provision of occupational information are worth examining. Kirton's study (1976) lead him to produce a job knowledge index (1979) which provides detailed information on a wide selection of jobs for the more able. The index asks whether a series of activities and facts about an occupation are true or false, and then provides the correct answers. This provides a good range of information about an occupation quickly and gives an individual the opportunity to assess how much they know. It also provides a useful basis for group work as well. The computer has provided the basis for two systems of providing occupational information. The Careers Literature and Information Prescription

Service (CLIPS) gives access to hundreds of items of occupational information. Pupils and parents can use the system to acquire a comprehensive selection of literature on occupations rapidly. The system is operated by the Careers Service in Bexley and Wiltshire and is likely to be adopted by other services. The other system, Job ideas and information generator-computer assisted learning (JIIG-CAL) provides information in two different ways. It will either print out brief or quite detailed summaries of job requirements and activities on demand or link these to an individual's profile which has been arrived at by completion of a questionnaire. JIIG-CAL has over 500 occupations in its data bank, covering the full ability range, and is updated regularly. The system will be described more fully in chapter seven.

The three main sources of occupational information are:

Careers Consultants Ltd., 12-14, Hill Rise, Richmond, Surrey.

Career and Occupational Information Centre (COIC), Manpower Services Commission, Moorfoot, Sheffield, S14 BR.

Careers Research and Advisory Centre (CRAC), Hobsons Press (Cambridge) Ltd., Bateman Street, Cambridge, CB2 1LZ.

Work Experience

Work experience is an activity within careers education that has had a rather uneasy history, although it has been seen as an important element in occupational choice for some years now. The Newsom report in 1963 recommended "limited experience of different kinds of employment, on a release-from-school basis, inside the educational programme". However, legal difficulties and some opposition by Trade Unions meant that it was not until the early seventies that work experience began to make any real impact. Even then, the Institute of Careers Officers estimated that in 1975/6 only 7% of school leavers had been involved in work experience schemes.

Work experience has several objectives. Prominent amongst these is informing youngsters of the world of work first hand, and hopefully motivating them more fully towards a job, as well as encouraging them to work harder at school to achieve their objective. A wider objective is that of increasing their knowledge and understanding of society, and preparing them for the transition from school to work. Subsidiary objectives have also existed in terms of using work experience as a means of helping youngsters get a job through contact with an employer, whilst some schools have used it as a way of getting rid of disruptive pupils for a while!

Watts (1983) reviews the variety of work experience schemes in existence. These range from the ambitious Project Trident, which operates nationally, using managers seconded from industry to coordinate and initiate schemes to school based approaches. Simulation exercises using school based production units and business games are also referred to by Watts, as well as the more traditional works visits. The Youth Opportunities programme had a work experience on employers premises scheme, as part of its offerings to unemployed youngsters. This clearly differed from school based schemes in a variety of important respects, and has now been superceded by the Youth Training Scheme. Work experience schemes have always relied heavily on the co-operation of employers, and the present recession is likely to make it more difficult to gain this co-operation. Added to this is the fact that the Youth Training Scheme does incorporate an element of more general 'job tasting', rather that just specific vocational training. In future, work experience may be transferred to the M.S.C. through its Y.T.S. and its New Technical and Vocational Education Initiative.

Careers Education and the Curriculum

'Careers Education in Secondary Schools' (1973) described two approaches to introducing careers education into schools. Firstly, by 'infusion', it is possible to construct a syllabus in a wide range of subjects that would deal with the world of work. Secondly, careers education is given space on the timetable as a subject in its own right.

Infusion takes several forms. For example, in 1975, the Schools Council published a geography programme for 14-16 year olds entitled 'People, place and work'. It examines work in terms of personal experience, Britain and the world. It asks "Why work"?, looks at patterns of work, changes in employment structures, how work affects the environment and the future of work. Its content is linked to programmes of study in English, Mathematics, Humanities, History and Careers Education. A selection of examples of infusion are described in the D.E.S. "Schools and Working Life". These range from cooperation between a firm and a school in the design of a leisure complex to the development of an 'O' level and CSE Chemistry course, that included work experience and a study based on industrial visits.

Another form of infusion that is growing in scale and importance is the use of time devoted to pastoral care, for careers work. Active Tutorial Work (1981) is a good example of this development. In most secondary schools, pupils have a personal tutor who spends some time with them each week. The use of this time, until recently, has not been formalised, or necessarily well organised. Active Tutorial Work provides a set of exercises for tutors to use, from year one to year five. The fifth year exercises include a number of self assessment activities, as well as finding out from the world of work, interviews and application forms. This development, linked to in-service training, has opened the way for many more teachers to become involved in careers work. This breaks down the artificial boundaries that have been constructed to separate academic work from pastoral care, from careers education and from the world outside. The field of 'life skills' work, as we have seen, is closely linked to careers education, and the growing emphasis on this, in social education within the school and beyond, in the Y.T.S. for instance, is an exciting development.

Evaluating Careers Education

Evaluating a complex phenomenon such as a careers education programme is no easy task, and is open to all sorts of errors. Careers education is not merely concerned with imparting knowledge and information, but is also dealing with values, attitudes and motivation. Indeed, some of the more valuable aspects of careers education may be very difficult to measure, such as increased ability to make decisions and greater self confidence or more self awareness. This is not to say that evaluation should not be attempted by those carrying out careers education and by professional researchers, but it does highlight some of the difficulties in drawing conclusions from what research is available. Finally, there is the added difficulty of time scale, as much of careers education is developmental and its 'fruits' may take some years to emerge.

Research and evaluation specifically of careers education is slight in this country as Clarke (1980) and Watts and Kidd (1978) testify. Hopson et al (1970) studied two year groups at a small secondary modern school. Little supporting evidence for the effectiveness of careers education emerges from this study, but overall the results are rather conflicting and difficult to interpret. However, the group who had followed the careers course did perceive school as having been more helpful in preparing them for the world of work. A more recent study by Chamberlain (1982) used a questionnaire to assess the 'career awareness' of 274 fifth form students from six different schools. His findings suggest that

1. Job knowledge possessed by students depends on their academic ability and the school they come from. Regular careers lessons tend to increase the job knowledge of average and below average students.

2. Whilst careers lessons themselves are not generally regarded as helpful sources of career knowledge, exposure to them changes the pattern of sources used by students. The lessons seem to encourage students to use a wider variety of sources and in particular to diminish their dependence on the family.

3. Students who have regular careers lessons are more aware of the preparations necessary for job interviews than are their peers.

Work experience is a small but important element of careers education, and Pumfrey and Schofield (1982) examined the impact of a school organised work experience scheme on the career maturity of 80 5th form pupils. An American instrument, Crites Career Maturity Inventory was used to measure differences between the group of 48 pupils who undertook work experience, and the 32 who did not. The inventory had a number of limitations, but despite this the results are of interest. Work experience had a significant effect on attitudes, self appraisal and occupational knowledge. In the case of three other variables, goal selection, planning and problem solving, it did not have a sgnificant effect. In the case of sex differences, the only significant difference was found in problem solving, whilst regards attainment, the only significant difference was found in the attitude scale.

Youthaid produced an interesting study of the transition from school to working life (1979). This study examined careers education amongst a whole range of other topics. The views of 250 school leavers, from 5 schools in London, Newcastle on Tyne and Northumberland were sought, as well as the views of careers teachers and careers officers in these schools. It is worth noting that although it was claimed that careers education was improving each year, if there was a timetable clash with examinable subjects, careers education was the first to go. Careers teachers were only able to devote a minority of their time to this function.

The youngsters were asked whether they had been told about wages, interview techniques and how to register as unemployed. In reply, 43%, 57% and 29% said "yes" to these topics. In response to these figures, Youthaid suggest that

> "much careers education, however well or badly implemented, is conceived as pastoral or quasi-psychotherapeutic (stressing decision making, personal and occupational development etc.) and this tends to be at the expense of hard informaton on the realities of the working world (and unemployment world). This may be partly because schools tend to operate as a closed system with limited links with the world of work outside. It may also be because the personal guardian and pastoral role is more appealing to teachers in terms of professional status than the mere transmission of factual information and technical skills". able to change the situation and fell back on marriage and having children as a means of "fulfilling themselves".

Work experience is something that pupils in

the Youthaid study wanted, and when it was offered the schools concerned were more popular with these leavers. When asked whether their last year at school had been a good preparation for working life, over half (55%) answered "no"; several months after leaving school, in answer to the same question, those saying "no" had risen to 69%. On being asked what they expected from their careers teacher at school, the majority said either "Tell me about working life", "Help me to get a job", or "Not much". The Careers Service emerges rather more favourably from this study, with 72% finding the Careers Officer helpful. This was equally true six months after leaving school, and the Careers Service was identified as the most useful source of advice in the future. Many careers officers commented that much of their interviews had to be devoted to 'disabusing young people of unreasonable aspirations', and in fact about one third changed their minds, having seen a careers officer. Youthaid commented that careers education and the careers officer's interview comes too late for many youngsters.

An earlier study by Thomas and Wetherall (1974) examined 96 schools, but only boys were included in the sample, (an unfortunate example of sexism). Careers officers were asked to rate the adequacy of careers provision in the schools. Only 18% were rated as completely adequate, whilst 38% were rated as inadequate; the remaining 44% were just about adequate. This is not surprising in view of the lack of time and resources allocated to careers work in the schools concerned. Only 40% of boys had received formal careers lessons, although a higher proportion had attended some careers activity, such as a careers convention, talk by the Armed Services, or a works visit. Nearly one in five of the boys was not aware that there was a careers teacher in his school, whilst three quarters said that they had never had a personal talk with their careers teacher. Contact between parents and the careers teacher was negligible.

The relationship between careers education and careers service interviews is important, and is one that emerges from a study carried out by the Dept. of Employment, Careers Service Branch (1982). The study, which involved almost 200 schools, and 680 pupils, showed that more progress was made in careers service interviews when pupils had attended a careers education course. Whether the careers officer participated in the careers education course does not seem to have mattered, but when the careers officer participated in the planning of the course, a higher proportion of interviews were rated 'above average' in effectiveness.

The nature of careers education and its effectiveness are obviously linked and earlier in this chapter various models were discussed. A study by West and Newton (1983) posed a number of fundamental questions about careers education. The findings are based upon a sample of 174 boys and girls at two schools. The careers teachers at these schools had different approaches to their work. At Woodbank, the careers teacher was a "vigorous proponent of the developmental approach", whilst at Brookvale, the careers teacher was more traditional, being concerned with finding jobs for his pupils. The initial occupational choices made by Woodbank pupils were aimed at jobs of higher status than those of pupils at Brookvale, and West and Newton attribute this to the careers education programme. When the actual jobs obtained are compared with original choices, it was found that Woodbank pupils attained jobs that were of lower status than the initial aspiration. The authors are critical of this, as they feel that pupils' aspirations were raised unrealistically high, and quote Roberts (1977) to support their view.

West and Newton launch into a vigorous attack on the developmental approach, which, they say, ignores the reality of unemployment and of boredom and drudgery in much work. Their argument loses some credibility when they contradict themselves by first saying that the developmental approach is applicable to the more able, but then say that this should not apply in practice because it promotes elitism. They make an interesting point that careers education, when it fosters self awareness, is out of step with the rest of education, which is concerned with learning facts. Having said this, West and Newton suggest that youngsters should be encouraged to examine their working conditions and make "constructive attacks" on them. They are saying that schools should not produce compliant, accepting pupils who are willing to go along with the existing divisions in society.

The study is also critical of the 'talent matching' approach to guidance which is described as paternalistic and unrealistic, in the sense that it is not really feasible. The youngsters in this study wanted more detailed information about jobs, and were keen to do work experience. The authors also make a plea for more help on how to cope with unemployment. Although West and Newton present an interesting and useful argument, they do not provide sufficient evidence to substantiate their conclusions about developmental careers education.

Employers are another group concerned with careers education. Jones (1983) reports that three quarters of her sample

> "remarked particularly on the inadequacy of the programmes, the lack of information given and the lack of qualified teachers involved. Another 15% singled out the importance of work experience, interview and form filling preparation and the need for more industrial involvement".

One of the most notable debates about careers education was carried out on the pages of the British Journal of Guidance and Counselling (vol.5 No.1.1977) between K. Roberts and P. Daws. The very different positions they adopt do represent fundamentally opposed views of careers education and the social context in which it operates. Robert's opportunity structure theory has been discussed in Chapter 3, and his views on careers education stem from this determinist view of how our society works. Put briefly, he maintains that a developmental careers programme that seeks to expand youngster occupational aspirations and encourages them to have 'unrealistic' ambitions, "leaves them less adaptable when faced with the constraints of job availability". He deduces from this that "careers work should concentrate upon practical employment problems", although he does not go into detail to explain what should be included and excluded in his careers programme.

He maintains that "careers officers dislike crisis counselling", and suggests that placement and follow up has been neglected, with the result that "unfavourable impressions of the Service inevitably follow". This last comment is not substantiated by various research studies which show a majority of youngsters satisfied in their dealings with the careers service, although a good deal less happy with the role the school has played in this transition period. This is an important distinction. The Careers Service, generally speaking, is professional in its approach to youngsters and employers. Whilst it has rightly tried to help develop careers education in school, it has not neglected its responsibilities in placement or follow up. This has been specially true with the advent of unemployment specialists who, by definition, do not work in schools. One has the feeling that despite the power of some of Roberts's arguments, he has not kept in touch with developments in the Careers Service as much as he should have done, since his research project in 1969.

Daws is highly critical of Roberts on a number of counts. He maintains that there is a lot more social and occupational mobility than Roberts accepts, and that individuals, however limited, do have more choice than he states. Daws fully supports the emphasis on self awareness of some careers programmes, on the grounds that it is a preparation forlife in general and not just for work. He states that the purpose of careers education programmes is to help children transcend socially-imposed barriers to a full awareness of choice and opportunity". They "seek to help children own themselves, to become autonomous, self directing and less vulnerable to social pressures". He concludes by stating that "guidance must also play the role of catalyst in the production of desirable social change. Suitably tackled, it can become an instrument of progressive rather than conservative social policy".

Summary

It has only been possible to touch upon a variety of issues relating to careers education in this chapter. In many respects, careers education can be seen as central to the process of occupational choice, and thus of crucial importance to those working in vocational guidance. Careers education has developed and changed considerably in the last decade, yet this process is clearly going to have to continue if it is to keep pace with developments in the outside world. Recently Geoffrey Holland, Director of M.S.C. stated that the advent of the Youth Training Scheme would signal a radical change in careers education and advice. He linked this specifically to the twelve occupational training families on which the Y.T.S. is based, indicating that young people will need to examine these, rather than individual jobs, as their initial starting points.

Watts, Law and Fawcett (1981) suggested that an "individual in community model for guidance" as an eclectic scheme offering a way forward for those working on vocational guidance. It has a good deal to offer those working in careers education and is worth examining in some detail. They state that "for the practitioner to imagine that somehow he or she can accept sole responsibility for guidance is a delusion". Following on from this, three roles are outlined; those of coordinator, innovator and counsellor. The coordinator needs to identify the full range of human resources inside and outside the school which play, or might play, a part in vocational guidance. Potentially, this is a long list and ranges from peer groups to employers, caretakers to trade unionists.

This is the philosophy underlying much of the work of the Schools Council Careers Education and Guidance project and ultimately has far reaching implications for the whole school. Innovation calls for intervention, which requires both boldness and imagination. Watts, Law and Fawcett suggest that although innovation does take place it is, for the most part, not backed by theory. More attention to in service training, both full-time and part-time, is certainly called for. Counselling has been discussed in the previous chapter and reference has been made to the range of 'consultancy skills' that can be applied. A 'second agenda' of finding out about the quality of help being offered in the 'guidance community' is suggested as an important adjunct to the normal counselling role. This links in with the counsellor's other two roles and helps him to monitor this 'guidance model'.

Chapter Seven

TESTS, QUESTIONNAIRES AND COMPUTER BASED GUIDANCE SYSTEMS.

"Test scores are only estimates of what a person can do on a limited set of tasks at a given time under a particular set of circumstances" Barry and Wolf (1962)

In a previous chapter, the early importance of tests and measurements to vocational guidance was stressed. This initial emphasis has not developed and grown, as might have been expected, in this country at least. However, instruments that attempt to measure, assess and match individuals are still an important part of vocational guidance and counselling. In fact, with the widespread applications of computers, this sort of instrument has gained a new lease of life, and it is fair to say that the computer offers considerable possibilities to those working in vocational guidance.

In this chapter it will be important to distinguish carefully between the various instruments available, because they vary considerably in their nature, purpose and application. It is worth emphasising this point as tests and questionnaires have sometimes been misunderstood and misused in vocational guidance. Holdsworth (1976) maintains that the most important reasons for using tests are objectivity and comprehensiveness. Appraisal by others is a part of life, but objective appraisal is a rare commodity and psychometric tests do offer some measure of objectivity. On the other hand, tests attempt to be comprehensive in the items they measure by means of good sampling.

Kline (1975) states that there are three criteria for good psychological tests - high reliability, high validity and good norms. Reliability has two meanings; internal consistency and reliability over time. Validity refers to the matter of how far the test measures what it purports to measure. The way in which a test is constructed may mean that it becomes a test of comprehension as much as a test of say, mechanical ability. The validity of a test has a number of different aspects to it. For instance, Kline points out that the face validity of a test is likely to be important where the full co-operation of the client is required. Clearly the predictive validity of a test is of considerable importance and is given great emphasis by most psychologists. Norms are the set of scores which make it possible to draw comparisons between subjects taking a test. Sampling, which leads to the establishment of norms, should aim to be representative of whatever group the test is going to apply to. Finally, a good test should produce a wide distribution of scores, thus providing a tool that is able to discriminate clearly between any group of individuals taking it.

Holdsworth (1976) gives three areas where tests and questionnaires can help in vocational guidance and counselling. These are:-

1. Highlighting strengths and weaknesses, likes and dislikes, personality characteristics etc. These provide an ipsative profile of the individual.

2. Assisting individuals to see how they measure up on any of these characteristics in comparison with other people. In other words, a normative measure.

3. Stimulating new ideas about the individual's attributes in some vocational or educational direction.

Tests.

Psychologists have devised tests to measure an almost endless range of human attributes. Kline (1982)quotes three leading figures in psychometrics. Guilford claimed there are 120 abilities, whilst Thurstone settled for nine primary abilities. Spearman, on the other hand, maintained that general reasoning ability alone was of prime importance. Hence, there is some disagreement about what needs to be tested in the area of ability alone, and this has resulted in a multitude of tests being devised.

The main groupings of abilities that have preoccupied psychometricians are:

1. Verbal - understanding of words and ideas.

2. Numerical - facility in manipulating numbers.

3. Spatial - ability to visualise two or three dimensional figures when their orientation has been changed.

4. Perceptual speed and accuracy - judging whether pairs of stimuli are similar or different.

5. Reasoning - involves induction from the specific to the general.

6. Memory - can mean short term recall or the linking of pairs in some meaningful way.

7. Word fluency - rapid production of words, conforming to a letter requirement, but without meaning.

The first three abilities have formed the basis for the majority of tests used in vocational guidance. Mechanical reasoning is an ability that has been of interest to psychometricians, as have musical and artistic abilities, although tests of these abilities have not been much used in vocational guidance. Testing psychomotor abilities has been more prominent however, with speed, control, coordination and judgement being particular factors that have been isolated.

In 1971, the Department of Employment Vocational Assessment Test (DEVAT) was introduced into the Youth Employment Service on an experimental basis. In 1977, a Dept. of Employment Survey showed that about 20,260 individuals were being tested annually by DEVAT. Although this is a very small proportion of all pupils receiving vocational guidance, DEVAT was still likely to be the main test instrument in use by the Careers Service. Lack of time and resources were given as reasons for the limited use of DEVAT. Since 1977, it is unlikely that the use of this test battery or other tests has increased, so it does mean that the majority of youngsters receiving vocational guidance from the Careers Service will not have been tested for aptitude, although many more of them will have completed some other sort of instrument such as an interest questionnaire.

DEVAT is a multi-aptitude battery of tests, made up of:

1. Arithmetic - measuring skills to perform arithmetic operations quickly and accurately (10 minutes).

2. Shapes - measuring the ability to judge relationships of shapes and to visualise and reorganise these shapes mentally (15 minutes).

3. Same Word - measuring the knowledge of the meaning of words (5 minutes)

4. Reasoning - measuring the ability to perceive and grasp the underlying relationship between a series of verbal and/or numerical symbols (15 minutes).

5. Mechanical - measuring the ability to understand and apply the principles underlying mechanics and to reason in practical situations (30 minutes).

6. Mathematics - measuring the range of mathematical knowledge and the ability to apply mathematical concepts speedily (10 minutes).

These six tests take about two hours in total to administer.

There are two further tests that are available for occasional use.

7. Clerical - measuring speed and accuracy in performing a simple clerical task (15 minutes).

8. Visual reasoning - measuring the ability to perceive and grasp the underlying relationship between a series of designs (20 minutes).

All the tests are paper and pencil tests, and are

aimed at the average school leaver, which means that the less able may well have problems in completing them. DEVAT's coverage compares quite closely with two other well known test batteries, the Differential Aptitude Test and the General Aptitude Test battery. With regard to the thinking behind DEVAT, it is worth quoting the manual (1975) which states that it "is perhaps more concerned with the developmental approach than with the employment interview approach." DEVAT was thus designed to increase pupil's self awareness and self assessment, rather than to categorise them into specific occupations.

The manual has a number of interesting comments to make about the role of testing in vocational guidance which apply more widely. Tests can be perceived as another sort of examination by pupils, and as a version of secondary school selection by parents and teachers. The counsellor must try to represent tests as being a part of vocational guidance and fitting into a programme of careers education. In fact the manual goes so far as to say that "tests should only be introduced if there is a reasonable careers activity in the school". Pupils should be fully aware of why and how tests are to be used.

The issue of who decides on the tests to be used, and if they are to be used is discussed in the manual. Goldman (1971) is quoted in regard to clients playing a part in test selection. He states that when this happens, there is less resistance to the testing itself, the tests chosen are likely to be more appropriate, the client has an opportunity to make a decision, and the discussion between client and counsellor can be a productive process in itself. In fact, when Price (1973) tested a group of 250 school leavers, it was found that only 70% of boys and 50% of girls found the experience useful, which suggests that had this group been given a choice, the proportion who found the experience of value might well have been higher. Clients playing a part in test selection has a number of clear advantages, but in reality, there is likely to be little choice of tests available beyond DEVAT.

When it comes to making use of the DEVAT results, the manual points out that the counsellor "may attempt to make use of his insights into and experience of the occupational world in order to make logical deductions from the test information".

Whilst accepting this, the manual goes on to add

> "that in the absence of criterion-related validity information, any interpretation based on logical analysis may well be incorrect. The counsellor must always be aware that any relationship he draws between tests and job performance remains an intuitive hypothesis".

DEVAT provides "a more accurately defined outline of abilities" for counsellor and client to use to construct hypothesis about likely jobs. The manual is quite clear in putting a joint responsibility on both counsellor and client to interpret the DEVAT results. It suggests that this is an important part of the interview process, i.e.

> "training the client to be able to cope more effectively and successfully with the problem of choosing a career, and this objective cannot be achieved if all of the skills are seen as the preserve of the counsellor".

The DEVAT manual has a number of other points to make about communicating test results to clients, which have general application. Test results should be studied prior to the interview to allow the counsellor to look for possible areas of discrepancy, for instance. It is important to note that "determination of general level is likely to be more accurate than the determination of any particular ability". The suggestion is made that the test results should be linked to discussion of school subjects, whilst at some point, the counsellor must find out how his client reacted to doing the tests. This is necessary, as test performance is dependent on factors such as motivation, understanding of the instructions, anxiety and physical fitness. It should be pointed out that his true score could be slightly higher or lower.

Tact is the keynote in communicating test results to clients and especially to their parents. The manual stresses that tests are " intended to enable client and counsellor to communicate more effectively, not to drive a barrier between them". Tests are only one source of information about any client and must be seen as such. They can take on a mystique which gives them a special status as scientific, objective and irrefutable information.

This mystique has, in part, been generated by some psychologists and by some counsellors who have seen tests as investing them with "professional power" and prestige. In this situation, clients can assume the status of objects to be measured, judged, classified and directed. Two final points; the manual emphasises using tests in a positive sense to bring out client's strengths, and it advises caution with the scores of 'immigrant' children, pointing out that "much will depend on how much English is spoken at home".

Interest questionnaires

There are many interest inventories, guides or questionnaires in existence, and which have been used in vocational guidance. Some, like the A.P.U. Occupational Interest Guide, have been used extensively by the Careers service, whilst others, like the Vocational Preference Inventory, (VPI) have been used very little in this country. Clarke (1980), in her critical review of U.K. research, mentions only one piece of research on an interest questionnaire, so there is a lack of thorough evaluation of these instruments in vocational guidance practice in Britain, although this is not true of the United States.

It is proposed to examine only a few of the better known and more interesting questionnaires. The first of these is the interest guide that forms part of the Job Ideas and Information Generator - Computer assisted learning (JIIG-CAL). The author of the system, Closs, originally devised the A.P.U. Occupational Interest Guide (O.I.G.), which by 1977, according to a Dept. of Employment Survey, was being used at the rate of 47,000 per annum, making it the most extensively used interest questionnaire in the Careers Service. JIIG-CAL will be discussed more fully later in this chapter, but it is appropriate to look at the guide separately as it can be, and is, used independently of the system as a whole.

Before doing this, it is worth spending some time in examining the nature of interests and their relevance to occupational choice. Kline (1975) claims that there is a good deal of confusion about the nature and meaning of interest tests. Closs (1980) has synthesised the views of five authors and produced a definition of interest which has much to commend it. Interests are characterised by a.) subjectivity - 'one man's meat is another man's poison'.

b.) a feeling of pleasure, which may be mild or intense, but must be present.

c.) being intrinsic to the activities in which it is experienced. This is the essence of interest, according to Closs. People have interests which are purely based on the activity itself and have nothing to do with the outcome necessarily.

d.) participation in these activities involving concentration of attention.

e.) the concentration of attention being comparatively effortless.

f.) activities which are interesting tend to involve a match of the individual's capacity and the demands of the activity. This suggests that there is a link between an individual's interests and his ability and temperament.

Closs goes on to add that interest is only one aspect of personality and is separate from, but related to, attitudes, needs and temperament. Interests are different from "motives of a more immediate nature in being of relatively long duration at relatively stable strengths". He continues by stating that occupational results are intrinsically no different from non-vocational interests. Closs maintains that vocational guidance needs interest questionnaires because many clients do not know how to order and interpret their interests in terms of choosing a job. The guide provides a structure which enables any individual's interests to emerge in a manner that is meaningful to both client and counsellor. In a very few instances, he or she may have no real interests, but this will be identified by the guide.

The guide is based on six different sections which care for the full range of ability and attainment. Pupils complete two adjoining sections. The sections are described in terms of

job level, e.g. semi-professional,
qualifications, e.g. 'A' levels needed,

training, e.g. about 3-5 years, and
study needed, e.g. full-time study often a part of the training.

The guide has six interest types which are described as follows:

Type 1 - Interest in practical work, making things with your hands and in science and engineering. Applies to woodwork, metalwork and also to mechanics, engineering science and physics.

Type 2 - People with this interest enjoy working with living things, which includes gardening, forestry, farming and looking after animals. Relates to science like medicine, biology and some kinds of chemistry.

Type 3 - Clerical, secretarial and saleswork, as well as administration and management. Includes economics and some aspects of law.

Type 4 - Neatness, tidyness and an eye for colour and shape are features. Includes cooking, dressmaking, pottery, weaving as well as fine arts.

Type 5 - Helping people in need, e.g. the old, children, the homeless.

Type 6 - Meeting and talking to people, e.g. entertaining, writing books, advising and guiding.

Closs states that there are three methods of response available to those constructing interest questionnaires; rating, ranking and paired comparisons. He decided to use two sorts of response, 'paired comparisons' and a rating scale of 'like--don't mind--dislike'. This appears to be unique amongst interest questionnaires, and provides two sets of responses which can be fruitfully compared and combined. The guide has sixty pairs comprising one hundred and twenty separate activities. It is not timed and can be hand scored by means of templates, as well as scored by computer.

Scores can be interpreted intuitively or by means of tables. The interest types are represented in two columns of six scores, which the counsellor and client examine and discuss in order to deal with any apparent discrepancies or response sets. Closs emphasises the need for joint interpretation of the interest scores in order to give the client a sense of involvement and to dispel any mystique the guide may have. The APU.O.I.G. operated on the same principle, although it had eight interest types and made up of two versions, one for those of average ability, and another for the older, more able. Unlike the guide that forms part of JIIG-CAL, it did not directly relate to occupations or provide suggested jobs.

John Holland's work has generated at least two well known interest inventories. His own Vocational Preference Inventory (VPI) dates back to 1953. It is a personality inventory composed of 160 occupational titles, which the client responds to by saying he likes or dislikes them. Holland claims that it yields "a broad range of information about the person's interpersonal relations, interests, values, self-conception, coping behaviour and identifications". The VPI has eleven scales, with the first six relating to Holland's six personality types, and the other five being self-control, masculinity, status, infrequency and acquiescence. Its most desirable use is a brief screening inventory and it is designed for persons of 'normal intelligence' over the age of 14.

Holland bases the VPI on a number of assumptions. Preference for an occupational title represents a number of things such as motivation, knowledge of the occupation, an understanding of himself and his abilities. People perceive occupational titles in stereotypes. Different occupations provide different sorts of satisfactions and require different abilities, values and attitudes. Accurate discrimination of different occupations is indicative of self understanding and maturity. Finally, Holland regards interest and personality inventories as serving the same purpose.

The VPI is self-administering and takes between 15 and 30 minutes to complete. No special training is required to administer or score it, but it should be interpreted by trained vocational counsellors. Holland lists a series of adjectives to describe males and a similar series to describe females in each scale. This is apparently based on empirical evidence. For each scale, there is a conceptual definition which "integrates the empirical and clinical experience and postulates the variable or variables represented by the scale".

These conceptual definitions are listed as follows:

Realistic:
Realism, practicality, masculinity, conventionality.

Intellectual:
Intellectuality, intelligence, unsociableness, rationality.

Social:
Sociability, femininity, passivity, problem solving by means of feeling, social responsiblity, introjection of moral standards and religious values.

Conventional:
Conformity, uncritical acceptance of cultural values and attitudes, obsessive orderly concern with rules, regulations, worrying.

Enterprising:
Dominance, risk taking, sociability and enthusiasm.

Artistic:
Artistic interest, anxiety and immaturity, expressiveness, originality, unconventionality, erratic behaviour and effort.

Self-Control:
Overcontrol of impulses - denial, passivity, repression.

Masculinity:
Masculinity - femininity cluster of variables which includes occupational roles, identification with males or females, conflicts with these identifications.

Status:
Concern for prestige and power, also self esteem.

Infrequency:
Taps a cluster of positively correlated traits, attitudes and deficiencies, i.e. self deprecation, incompetence, socially undesirable traits. Holland talks about this scale being a social desirability scale and also indicating "social, vocational and intellectual deviancy" at one end and "normalcy and effective functioning" at the other end. This does raise some important issues regarding the values and judgemental qualities being expressed by Holland. It also applies to his masculinity scale and the split between males and females in the empirical summary.

Acquiescence:
The main value of this scale is to detect extreme response biases which can go undetected in forced choice tests.

Holland is fairly brief in his instructions on how to interpret the profiles that emerge from his inventory. He points out that for example one should expect a high score on the status scale if there is a high score on the enterprising scale, whilst there should be correspondingly low scores on the realistic and intellectual scales. There are three broad areas to consider

a.) Vocational interests and adjustment.

What is the subject's primary field of vocational interest? This is reflected in the first six scales. Are the remaining scales in the profile consistent with the six scales?

b.) Life Style

What are the three or four highest or lowest scales? These represent the favoured and rejected methods of "adaptive behaviour". Is the profile pattern integrated and consistent? What is the subject's typical mood? This can be judged by the acquiescence, social and enterprising scales.

c.) Personal effectiveness

Does the subject have desirable self control?

> This is reflected in the acquiescence and self control scales. Does the subject have high aspirations and a customary perception of the world? Low infrequency and high status scores will reflect this. What is the quality of the subject's interpersonal relations? Low social and enterprising scores with spontaneity and exuberance. Does the subject have any gross signs of behaviour disorder? These include high infrequency scores, extreme acquiescence scores and various other indicators. Does the person show potential for original or creative behaviour?

The V.P.I. has been administered to a wide range of people in the States, and this has provided a lot of normative data. As yet there is not comparable data available in this country, which restricts its use to experimental purposes, for the time being. Brentall (1982), a careers officer, administered the inventory to 341 pupils in Norwich. The statistics that emerged did show certain similarities with Holland's data, which is encouraging. He also did a comparative study of the VPI and OIG by administering both instruments to a group of 41 fourth year boys and girls. At the end of each inventory, each pupil completed a brief questionnaire asking for their reactions. Both emerged as useful, although Brentall points out that the VPI is much cheaper, is quicker to administer, and to mark.

The Strong Campbell Interest Inventory (SCII) is the other instrument that uses Holland's theory. The version that will be examined here is the British edition of the merged form of the Strong Vocational Interest Blank (SVIB) which was produced by David Campbell. The SVIB was first published in 1927, and Campbell has used this as the basis for the SCII, which merges the men's and women's forms and introduces Holland's theoretical framework. The SCII gives three main types of information. Firstly, on the six general occupational themes of Holland's - realistic, investigative, artistic, social, enterprising and conventional. Secondly, on 23 basic interest scales which report the consistency of interests or aversions. Thirdly, scores on 124 occupational scales, which show the degree of similarity between the respondent's interests and the characteristics of men and women, in a wide range of occupations.

The quesionnaire itself is a formidable document consisting of seven parts and a total of 325 items, and takes about 30 minutes to complete. Campbell (1977) claims that most pupils from aged 14 upwards are able to complete it. However, it does need to be machine marked and is relatively expensive, which makes its use in the public sector unlikely. The seven parts consist of the following items:

1. Occupations - 131 job titles.

2. School subjects - 35 subjects.

3. Activities - 50 items which include interests, job activities and things like living in a city.

4. Amusements - 38 items that include interests, and places of entertainment.

5. Types of people - 23 items covering a wide range of groupings. (The respondent is asked to indicate whether he likes, is indifferent to, or dislikes the items in the first five parts.)

6. Preference between two activities - 29 pairs of items which are either activities or occupational titles. In this case, the respondent makes one or other of the paired items or indicates that he can't decide.

7. Your characteristics - 13 items of behaviour, with the respondent indicating if they do, or don't describe them, or is they can't decide.

When interpreting the inventory profile the counsellor should point out its limitations and try to use it in a context which ought to include a wider programme of careers education and exploration. Initially, the counsellor checks the administrative indexes. These show total response, infrequent response and the proportions of like, dislike and indifferent responses for the different sections. If these responses deviate very much from the norm, it will be necessary to check this with the client. In doing so, some interesting reactions to the subject matter of the inventory and about the client may emerge.

The special scales are introversion/extroversion and academic orientation. The first measures the person's sociability to some extent, but should be treated with caution, whilst the second gives a rough guide as to the level of academic committment. The ultimate objective of the SCII is to arrive at a final code type. This is achieved by looking at the scores on the General Occupational themes, the interest scales, and the occupational scales. The final code type will indicate the first, second and possibly third personality type of Holland. Campbell concludes by making some cautionary comments about the use of the profile. "If the profile is used to push people in stereotyped, outmoded directions, it is worse than no help at all."

Self Help Instruments

Holland and Gottfriedson (1976) advocate the extensive use of self help instruments on the grounds that "most people can resolve vocational questions if they are provided with a rich climate of information and exploratory reinforcement". In this situation, individual counselling and guidance "becomes the treatment of last rather than first resort". In fact, they maintain that impersonal forms of help, either by computer or paper, work well because person to person counselling can sometimes hinder decision making on the part of the client, and does heavily depend on the sort of relationship that is established.

Holland devised a self directed search (SDS), and an occupations finder (OF), which provide a matching procedure. The SDS begins with occupational day dreams, where the subject is asked to list jobs that they have day dreamed about. They then proceed to an activities section, made up of six sub-sections, reflecting Holland's six personality types; realistic, investigative, artistic, social, enterprising and conventional. There are eleven activities in each sub-section, and the subject has to indicate whether they like or dislike them. Competencies come next, with again eleven items under each of the six sub-sections, with the subject having to say yes or no as to whether they can do them well or not.

The fourth section deals with occupations, and has the same six sections, with 14 job titles under each one. The subject has to indicate whether they find them interesting or not. Self estimates about the subject's abilities is the next section. Twelve abilities (two for each of Holland's types) are listed and the subject has to rate themselves on a seven point scale. The subject is asked to score the sections and, as a result of all these scores, a summary code based on the highest of the six personality types emerges.

This summary code can then be used to scan the occupations finder. This contains 500 jobs, divided into six sections; realistic (R), investigative (I), artistic (A), social (S), enterprising (E), and conventional (C), which are then sub-divided into a number of sub-sections. These sub-sections relate to the summary codes. For example, Artistic occupations has six sub-sections, with the following summary codes: ASE, ASI, AES, AIS, AIE, AIR, and a total of 39 job titles. Against each of the 500 occupations is a number from 1-6 which indicates the necessary educational level required to enter that occupation. In this way, the subject can progress through self assessment to job matching. However, the instruments do stress that the summary code is only an estimate, and that once some occupations have been identified, the subject should find out more about them before making any decisions. Both the SDS and OF need to be "anglisized" before they can be usefully used in Britiain.

The Quick job-hunting map was devised by Richard Bolles, who has produced a number of other longer works on occupational choice. The map is based on Holland's six personality types. Bolles uses this as a framework to sort out individual's functional and transferable skills. This is done by asking the subject to select up to seven of their most satisfying accomplishments, jobs or roles which are then considered in relation to a long list of skills. The skills come under a number of headings:

1. Machine or manual: athletic, outdoor or travelling.

2. Detail, follow through; Numerical, financial, accounting.

3. Influencing, persuading; performing; leadership; developing, planning, organising,

executing.

4. Language, reading, writing, communicating, instructing, interpreting, guiding, serving, helping, human relations.

5. Intuitional and innovating; artistic.

6. Observational, learning; research, investigating, analysing, evaluating.

When this is complete, the subject needs to look at patterns and priorities. Patterns emerge when considering how often particular skills are used, whilst priorities will depend on the subject deciding on which skills they want to use most. Bolles suggests using a grid to help decide on priorities. Whilst focusing on transferable skills, Bolles does not ignore other factors playing a part in job hunting. He encourages the reader to consider the location of the job, what special knowledge it requires, what sort of people he wants to work with, the sorts of values and purposes linked to work, working conditions, and finally the level of responsibility and salary.

The Quick job hunting map is more suitable for those who have some working experience, than the school leaver. This group have less easy access to vocational guidance and therefore a self-help device of this kind serves a real need. The Open University have recognised this and published a similar sort of booklet for use by their students. Bolles is not trying to match people to specific jobs as Holland does, with his SDS and OF. His map is more concerned with increased self awareness and with boosting confidence by showing that we all have skills and that these skills have wider application than we recognise.

It is interesting to note that the Youth Training Scheme is centred around the notion of transferable skills which is now so necessary at a time when there is much less job security than a few years ago. The division between work and non-work skills is artificial to a large extent, and both adults and youngsters need to be made aware of the notion of "Life skills" which are essential for functioning effectively, whether at work, at play or at home. The next decade will see a much greater emphasis on 'life skills' teaching in school, post school education and at work.

Computer Based Guidance.

The last decade has seen the development of a number of computer based guidance systems. Two of the best known systems will be examined in some detail, and mention will be made of some of the other systems that have been developed.

1. Job Ideas and Information Generator-Computer Assisted Learning (JIIG-CAL)

Reference has been made to this system earlier in this chapter, when considering the O.I.G., which is part of the overall system. JIIG-CAL developed from a merger of the APU Interest Guide, first published in 1969, and a computer assisted learning package used in the London Borough of Havering. It has three components;

the occupational interests guide,
the jobfile and
the computer programs.

The OIG is based on the subject's responses to 60 pairs of job related activities, which produces a profile of the subject's interests.

Having completed this guide, which takes about 35 minutes, it is then marked by computer and returned about a week later, allowing time for discussion of the profiles. The next step is to complete a further series of questions on working conditions, training, personal talents, priorities, school subjects and health. Each question is explained more fully in an accompanying illustration booklet. Again about 35 minutes is required for this exercise. The answer sheets are collected and marked by computer. A week later, a print out for each subject will be available, as well as a separate copy for the adviser or counsellor.

The subject's copy will normally list 20 jobs, with the following details for each job:

a.) Points rating 1 - 9, the higher rating indicating greater suitability.

b.) Short description of the job.

c.) Details of qualifications required.

d.) Short list of the main skills.

e.) Reference to relevant careers information, plus any important notes.

Two other printouts are available to the subject. The mini-print lists more than twenty jobs, whilst the maxi-print gives full and detailed information about specific jobs. This follows the same pattern as the normal print, but provides more information about job requirements and necessary skills.

The adviser's print contains detailed information about the subject's responses to the second part of the guide, showing whether he liked, disliked, or was neutral to each of the 87 items as well as listing his prioirities and any jobs affected by disabilities. The twenty jobs are also listed with their points ratings. JIIG-CAL can be used on its own as a matching device providing job suggestions and information, but Closs and his colleagues stress the desirability of integrating it into a careers education programme.

JIIG-CAL is sufficiently flexible to allow for this sort of integration. It is suggested that the second term of the 4th year is a good time to introduce it. At this stage, a letter to parents explaining that their children will be using the system is advised. The guide can be completed in class groups, but groups of 12-15 are recommended for feedback sessions. It requires between 6 and 8 periods to complete the whole system.

The Jobfile is not a vacancy file, but contains coded and descriptive information on over 500 occupations at all levels. The information is based on a wide range of published careers literature, supplemented by research carried out by JIIG-CAL staff. It is reviewed and updated regularly. Jobs are allocated to one of the same six sections or levels that apply to the guide, although a few jobs have to be included in more than one section, because of the different qualifications, training etc. required. It is possible to add local information to the system, which gives the system considerable potential flexibility.

By mid-1983, 28 LEA's, 3 technical colleges and 1 University were using the system, with 47,136 individual users in total in 1982. An increasing number of schools within registered LEA's are using JIIG-CAL, as more teachers are trained to use the system. The system is becoming more widely adopted each year and seems to have an ensured future, despite the relatively high costs involved. Amongst future developments of the system to be included is subject choice, and its relevance to later occupational choices. A large scale evaluation of the system is taking place and its results will be available in the near future.

(For further information about JIIG-CAL, contact the JIIG-CAL project, Edinburgh University, Business Studies Dept., 50 George Street, Edinburgh EH8 9JY).

2. Careers Advisory Service Computer Aid(CASCAID)

The system dates back to 1969 when 2 careers officers in Leicestershire, Witherspoon and Roberts conceived CASCAID. In 1975 three major decisions were made. First, it was decided to confine the system to pupils of above average academic ability, i.e. 3 'O' levels plus, because the less able had problems with vocabulary. In addition, for the less able, there was the problem of a databank of local jobs. Secondly, direct questions would be asked about the student's attitudes and feelings towards occupations, and that the answers would be accepted at face value. Finally, CASCAID would be available 'on line' as well as 'batch made'. From 1978, the system has been available nationally. Currently, 76 Careers Services and the Independent School Careers Organisation have CASCAID Mark V, with a total of 50,000 pupils using the system each year. There is a higher education version which is being used by 50 institutions, with about 6-8 thousand students making use of it, annually.

The subject completes a questionnaire for CASCAID Mark V, by first giving details of examinations taken, and to be taken. The system allows up to twelve variations of potential and actual academic qualifications and prints out these variations. There are then 80 items of occupational activities or working conditions on a 5 point scale to respond to. In addition, up to six of these items can be selected as key preferences. There are more short sections on further study, health factors and careers being considered by the client. The subject is asked to answer a series of questions which are not fed into the computer, but are used by the Careers Officer at the interview. These deal with employment experience, applications to further or higher education, leisure activities, and any special factors. There is also space for parents' comments.

The information is coded and fed into the computer, which matches it against a 'job bank' of over 400 titles. Print outs for the subject and for the Careers Officer are produced. The print outs contain a lot of information. For instance, it distinguishes between what are the essential, the prominent and the subsidiary aspects of the work. It warns about highly competitive entry, when health disabilities are a disadvantage, if study options conflict with the usual entry route; when the subject's qualifications are above average for the occupation, and if vocational/craft subjects are required.

The print out carries this sort of information in regard to occupations being considered by the subject, and also jobs selected by the system. In the latter case, a 'good match' of occupations which deserve 'serious consideration' are listed, followed by a 'fair match' of occupations which could be 'satisfactory'. Finally there are details of further information on all the occupations listed. There is a reference handbook for CASCAID which provides more information on the occupations in the system.

CASCAID is a system designed for use by the Careers Service, so it is not surprising that it emphasises the role of the Careers Officer in discussion of the print out. It stresses that the occupations listed by the computer are "suggestions, not recommendations". To quote "The system derives its rationale from the interview situation where the adviser needs to compare a mass of employment and education information with the interests and abilities of the client in order to make suggestions of suitable careers. It should not be confused with psychometric tests which try to discover innate traits, nor is it dependent on any particular guidance theory". CASCAID does emphasise the active participation of the subject in discussion of the print out. This is important as systems of this nature can induce a passivity, best summed up by a feeling that the computer has "deliberated" and "decided" on suitable occupations, and therefore must be correct.

The CASCAID - HE system produces a similar print out, but is based on 200 'graduate' occupations. The questionnaire is different, having 93 items of occupational activities or working conditions, but has the same five point scale with provision for up to 6 key preferences. There is a section on physical features and one on careers considered. Similarly, there is a section asking for informaton which is not entered into the computer. This asks about aspects of work not covered in the questionnaire and about personal factors which may influence choice of occupation.

CASCAID has not been formally validated or evaluated which is surprising in view of the length of time it has been in operation. The CASCAID Unit at Leicester are investigating students perceptions and feelings towards items in the questionnaire as well as continuing to analyse the occupations in the 'job bank'. There seems to be a relative lack of resources to provide the sort of research into the system that JIIG-CAL has received. This is something that needs to be rectified.

(For further information about CASCAID, contact CASCAID Unit, West Annex, County Hall, Glenfield, Leicester. LE3 8RF).

3. Job Match

Job Match was written and researched by the Industrial Training Research Unit (ITRU) and is geared to the non-academic school leaver. It involves the subject completing an 'ask yourself' questionnaire of 49 questions, taking about 15-20 minutes. This can be done manually, or by interaction with a computer. If done manually, hand marking is rather laborious and takes another 15 minutes. The subject's scores are then matched against the forty jobs covered by the system. Once a number of jobs have been identified, the subject reads about them in an "inform yourself" booklet, which devotes a page to each occupation. On each page, there is information about what the job involves, the preferences of a sample of those working in the occupation, details of qualifications, training and where to get further information. There are at least two photographs of people at work, in the occupation, on each page. The photographs attempt to get away from both sexual and racial stereotyping.

The 'ask yourself' questionnaire uses questions relating to working conditions. This covers four main ideas; Physical environment which includes accident risk and working outdoors. Social Environment which includes the sort of people one works with. Work Content which includes tools used, and the nature of the task, and finally Working Method which includes variety, autonomy, etc. Norms for the 40 occupations were derived from a sample of 1084 young male workers and 801 young female workers. There were considerable differences between male and female response patterns. This resulted in two sets of general scores for each job profile. "Males saw themselves as tough, aggressive and dynamic, females saw themselves as weak, comfort loving, and social. Despite these differences however, scores of male workers on corresponding female job profiles and vice versa are consistently high, indicating that job differences are greater than sex differences".

The authors of Job Match stress that it "should not be seen as a predictor, either of the particular job to which they would be suited or of their ability and aptitude to perform it". Having said this, it is not unreasonable to expect youngsters to see the exercise in just that way and it probably requires a good deal of careful explanation to dispel this illusion. Yet again the process seems important as the end result, and this needs to be explored by the counsellor. Like the other two systems, Job Match is not intended to be a substitute for either one to one counselling, or for careers education.

4. Other Computer Based Guidance Systems

The Interactive Careers Guidance System (ICGS) was developed in 1973 by IBM and Cheshire County Council. Unlike JIIG-CAL and CASCAID, it is a learning system, helping students to make career decisions. It also matches people to occupations, but operating from a smaller number of occupations than the other two systems. Being interactive, ICGS allows the student to use the system on their own, which has been shown to be favoured by the users. The system was field tested in two Cheshire schools, but has not developed beyond this.

Gradscope is a system designed for use exclusively in Higher Education. It was begun in

1975, funded jointly by the Science Research Council and the Association of Graduate Careers Advisory Services, and developed by Linda Wilson. Although an interactive version is now available, Gradscope normally operates on the basis of a completed questionnaire being coded and put into a computer, with a print out being returned in a few days time. The subject is asked to respond to 50 items distributed in three sections, dealing with work activities, e.g. advising or acting for members of the public; abilities and skills required in the work, e.g. communicating clearly and effectively in speech and conditions of work, e.g. good job security once appointed. Responses are on a five point scale, with the option of weighting certain items.

There are about 116 occupations in the databank and 8 to 12 occupations are printed out for the subject, as being most likely to interest him/her. Relevant information leaflets are referred to and the number of factor choices that have most influenced the results are given. The Careers Adviser also has a print out for each subject, which provides slightly more information. The system does not include occupations which specify a particular degree subject, and it does emphasise the desirability of discussing the print out with a Careers Adviser.

Finally, mention must be made of MAUD (Multi Attribute Utility Decompostion), which is the result of a research project into decision making and aiding. Wooler and Lewis (1982) have produced a system which operates on an interactive basis but with no data base. It works in a series of stages. The subject is asked to specify the occupations he is considering, then to elicit attributes relevant to these occupations by presenting them in triads and ask the student to specify differences and similarities between them. This is very similar to Kelly's Repertory Grid Technique. The subject then has to identify 'ideal' factors on the scales of these dimensions and to weight the dimensions as well, then feeding back the preferences. Subjects are encouraged to modify their input information in order to see the difference it makes. Wooler and Lewis have produced another system which presents a hierarchy of core factors to the subject, and asks him to weight them. This can be related to a number of occupations of interest to the subject and a preference ordering based on the hierarchy and the subject's responses will be produced. Both systems offer a lot of flexibility and are different from other systems as they lay emphasis on the process, rather than the content of decision making.

Repertory Grids

Repertory grids were first devised by Kelly (1955) as a means of applying his Personal Construct theory. They have been used in a number of contexts to help individuals increase their self awareness and make decisions. Their use in vocational guidance has been rather limited, although potentially they are a flexible device which can help counsellors to operate more effectively.

Smith, Hartley and Stewart (1978) set out a number of stages to be applied in using a repertory grid in vocational guidance. Firstly, it is necessary to establish the occupations that the subject might enter. The list should be between 12 and 20, so some encouragement may be necessary, in order to get a viable number of occupations to work with. Secondly, the subject's constructs need to be listed. These constructs are the qualities that people use to differentiate between the occupations "They are the lenses through which we perceive the objects of our world". The constructs can be elicited by using cards with one of the occupations written on it. Three cards are selected at random, and the subject is asked to say which of the two occupations are similar in some way, and to describe this way, e.g. accountancy and work with computers - might elicit the construct "well paid". This process of eliciting constructs continues in the same way using all the occupations until the subject has finished.

The next step is to cast the occupations against the constructs to form a grid. The subject is then asked to rate each occupation on each construct using a 5 or 7 point scale. The grid can be analysed by computer or visually in discussion between the subject and the counsellor. Smith, Hartley and Stewart used a program that gave a principal component analysis of the grid which allowed the construction of 'cognitive maps'. They also got their subject to rate his real self and his ideal self on each construct which gives some very useful information.

Edmonds (1979) discusses the limited use of repertory grids in the now defunct Occupational Guidance Units. He makes a case for their use in vocational guidance, stressing the point that no long training or special enterprise is necessary in order to use them.

Conclusion

The description and discussion of these tests and questionnaires has not been with the intention of enabling or persuading the reader to use them. The intention has been to highlight the use of such instruments in vocational guidance and counselling, and to discuss fairly briefly the nature of some of the more commonly used instruments in this country. There are various problems associated with the use of these instruments. They cost money, require training, and take time to administer and to interpret. Some of them require validation in this country. Thus it is perhaps not surprising that it is only in the private sector of vocational guidance, that such instruments have been used consistently.

Holdsworth (1976) recommends counsellors to be discriminating in their use of these instruments, by looking closely at the purpose for which they were designed, the population for which they were intended, and the committment to the instruments by those who designed them, i.e. how well were they validated? Those using tests should also be keenly aware that however objective these instruments attempt to be, when they are used, social factors impinge on the results. For instance, Watson (1972) showed that black children score higher when tested by a black person as opposed to being tested by a white person. King (1974) states that "the sex roles assigned to each sex are likely to have implications for attitudes to testing generally. It appears that the general direction of differential development of boys and girls is that boys are trained to be achieving, independent and self sufficient, whereas girls are trained to be group dependent, submissive and helpful to others. We may assume, if such training is successful that the demand placed on an individual by psychological testing will be more readily borne by boys, than by girls".

Hudson (1968) introduced the terms 'converger' and 'diverger' into testing terminology to illustrate the effect that different personality types can have upon performance in conventional psychological tests. He linked high performance in intelligence tests with factors such as specialism in the physical sciences, conventional attitudes, pursuit of technical interests in sparetime and emotional inhibition to describe his 'convergers'. His 'divergers' excelled at open ended tests, specialised in arts or biology, held unconventional attitudes, had interests connected in some way with people and were emotionally uninhibited. Whilst accepting that these are broad stereotypes of personality, Hudson's work has served the important function of showing that psychological tests have considerable limitations and accordingly, counsellors should be cautious in using and interpreting the results of any psychometric measure.

Barry and Wolf (1962) support this caution, by making a number of pertinent points about intelligence tests. They point out that a single test gives an incomplete picture of intellectual functioning (Batteries such as DEVAT attempt to overcome this, but inevitably even their scope is still limited). The fact that test scores are never absolute, but always estimates needs to be added. Tests inevitably 'test' other factors such as motivation to take tests which they are not designed to do and which affect their results. Tests also deteriorate with age. Finally, tests do not measure as accurately at the extremes as they do in the middle.

Barry and Wolf also have some reservations about interest inventories in vocational guidance. They point to research which maintains that interests are unstable in adolescence and hence are not good predictors of occupational success. The lack of relationship between ability and interest that can occur is also a problem. Finally, they suggest that the more able and gifted have many interests they wish to pursue, but interest inventories tend to narrow and limit these interests.

Computer based matching systems such as CASCAID and JIIG-CAL have begun to make a substantial impact on the practice of vocational guidance in the U.K. where psychometric tests and interest inventories have, to date, failed to do so. This is probably due to a number of factors. For instance, the computer based systems are 'packages' which can be administered on a large scale more simply and cheaply than test batteries and interest inventories. It also seem likely that the systems offer a 'talent matching' approach of a kind that appeals to those in vocational guidance influenced by the Seven Point Plan. There is the attraction and mystique of using the 'new technology' as well!

Chapter Eight

UNEMPLOYMENT AND THE FUTURE OF VOCATIONAL GUIDANCE

"Henceforth the quality of a society and of its culture will depend on the status of its unemployed: will they be the most representative productive citizens or will they be dependents?"
Illich (1978)

The subject of unemployment has inevitably come to dominate the work of those in vocational guidance in recent years. The signs are that this will continue to be the case for the forseeable future, thus it is appropriate to devote this final chapter to a discussion of unemployment. The discussion will examine the reasons for unemployment among the young, and its apparent impact upon their lives. The question of how education is coming to terms with unemployment will be considered and there will be an examination of the special measures established to deal with youth unemployment. Finally, the likely future of vocational guidance will be discussed.

The risk of unemployment is much greater closer to the school leaving age and continues to be high up to the mid-twenties. Despite the Youth Opportunities Programme, 22.6% of the labour force, under 18, were registered unemployed in January 1982, as opposed to 12.7% of the population as a whole. Young people without qualifications, who are more likely to come from working class families, are most at risk. The evidence also shows that girls and black youngsters are more liable to be unemployed than white boys. Radical changes in the occupational structure have contributed to this overall pattern. Many of the jobs traditionally reserved for teenagers have disappeared, e.g. messenger boy. There has been a long term decline in the number of apprenticeships. In 1968, 236,000 apprenticeships were offered, whilst in 1982 the figure had declined to about 100,000. Higher pay rates for the young has also led employers to prefer older workers, who are now available much more readily.

This has resulted in a downward shift in occupational expectations with many graduates entering jobs traditionally filled by those with lower qualifications. This pattern is working its way "down the system", thus affecting all those first entering full time employment. During the last decade, there has been a growing supply of young people leaving education and a declining demand for them. At the same time, the economic activity rates of married women increased substantially, as well as fewer people reaching retirement age due to the trough of births during the First World War. Structural changes in the economy have also had an impact. A substantial decline in employment in manufacturing and construction have particularly affected 16 year old male first entrants, whilst reductions in the service sector have affected many girls.

Young workers change jobs more frequently than adults, and thus run a higher risk of unemployment between jobs. These changes were in most cases voluntary, and not the result of sacking. Dissatisfaction with their present job was the principal reason. Raffe (1983), surveying a sample of nearly 900 qualified Scottish school leavers found that 40% left their first job within a year of leaving school. High youth unemployment did not deter them. A majority of them either mentioned their dislike of the job which they left or referred to a better opportunity which they hoped to take its place. Raffe comments that "it was more a product of occupational than of personal causes, more of unstable jobs than of unstable workers". Rees and Gregory (1981) show that long term unemployment i.e. over a year amongst the under 20's increased by 15% from 1970 to 1979. This rate of increase was much higher than amongst older age groups.

Casson (1979) draws attention to statutory school leavers as being particularly vulnerable to unemployment. For the most part, this group are the less able, less well qualified and most lacking in "employability skills". Figures (Table 8.1) for entrants to Youth Opportunities Schemes support this view.

However, the table also shows the growing number of better quaified entrants to Y.O.P.s schemes in 1981 and 1982. The proportion of girls on Y.O.P. fell from 50% to 47% (1979-82). There was a wide variation in the number of black youngsters on Y.O.P., reflecting their varying distribution in the country, as a whole. In London (1981/2), about half those on Y.O.P.s schemes were black. Regional variations are considerable, as would be expected. The Midlands had the highest number of youngsters on Y.O.P.s schemes, with 20% of the total for England and Wales. London had the least, with 4% of the total.

Table 8.1
Educational qualifications of Entrants to Y.O.P. 1978/82 (Source = SPD)

	No qualif'ns	%	Some CSE below Gr.1	%	CSE Gr.1/ 'O' Level	%	Total
1978/79	79500	49	40500	25	42200	26	162000
1979/80	97400	45	65000	30	54000	25	216400
1980/81	126000	35	126000	35	108000	30	360000
1981/82	166000	30	193500	35	193000	35	553000

Roberts et al (1982) conducted a study of over 500 16-20 year olds living in 4 areas of high unemployment in England. Three quarters had experienced unemployment at some stage since leaving school, which in effect meant that it was "rarely socially isolating or experienced as a stigma". The sample were usually employed in non skilled manual work or special measures, which lasted on average 9 months. Departure was mainly voluntary.

> "The young unemployed have never anchored their identities to particular occupations, their spells of joblessness are usually brief and they can realistically expect their prospects to improve with time".

Roberts et al describe this state as 'subunemployment'. These youngsters were selective in what they were prepared to apply for because "rejections can be painful, a greater threat to self-confidence than joblessness itself". They found unemployment boring and lacked money, but regarded it as a break between work. Roberts et al claim that unemployment is structurally inevitable, and state that "they are competently educated and counselled to cope with unemployment, albeit by families, peers and education's 'hidden curriculum', rather than through the deliberate efforts of statutory agencies".

Youngsters become "acquiescent rather than rebellious" for the most part. Although this was broadly true of this sample, there were those younsters who felt cheated at not being able to get better jobs which had been suggested by school and the Careers Service. This was particularly true of the black youngsters in the survey. Many had ambitions and supportive parents who expect a better deal for their children, than they had themselves. This resulted in many black youngsters being labelled as "unrealistic" by the Careers Service. Having said this, 2/3 of the sample who gave any opinion expressed satisfaction with the Careers Service. Roberts et al discuss the problems Careers Officers face in coping with the problems that "those who can match their client's ambivalence will be most likely to establish rapport with the young people they are able to assist".

Unemployment and Schools

In an earlier chapter, the role that schools adopt with regard to unemployment was discussed, especially in terms of careers education. In particular, the views of Watts (1978) were examined. He identified a number of curricular objectives relating the issue of unemployment and concluded that most schools have not dealt with it seriously. He explained this in several ways. Teachers felt that they could not deal with unemployment as they lacked first hand experience. It was also seen as highly political and emotive. There was also a feeling that by raising the issue of unemployment the 'work ethic' within the school would suffer accordingly. Finally, there was an instinctive hostility to the idea of "preparing youngsters for unemployment on the grounds that this was prejudging them".

These explanations were confirmed by Fleming and Lavercombe (1982) who found the emphasis in schools was on job hunting, although this emphasis was questioned by some careers staff. From discussions with teachers, careers officers and youth workers, the following points emerged. Some basis for self respect for the unemployed needs to be encouraged, although this raises some fundamental issues about social attitudes. Youngsters need to be 'educated' to use their time when unemployed as enjoyably as possible. The practical details of claiming benefits should be made clear. Educational opportunities beyond school ought to be explained and finally, discussion of the political and economic reasons for unemployment should be encouraged.

Seabrook (1983) maintains that "nothing is demanded of the young (working class) but their continued passivity and quiescence. Nothing is asked of them. They seem to have no place in the world, except as obedient and abject competitors for all that is tantalizingly held out to them. And the real choice is obscured from them - the possibility of another context in which this would not be so. In this way, the primary determinant in their lives has been, not work, not doing or contributing or creating anything but the lopsided insistence on buying, getting and having".

Jahoda (1982) has identified five aspects of being unemployed that leads to psychological deprivation. These are a lack of time structure to life, and the reduction of social contacts. The lack of participation in collective purposes and the absence of regular activity were two other factors. Finally, there was an absence of an acceptable status and its consequences for personal identity. Schools can help youngsters become aware of these consequences and to some degree, suggest ways of coming to terms with them. However, other agencies such as the Careers Service, Centres for the Unemployed, and Self-Help groups are needed to help youngsters cope with the stresses of unemployment.

Current school attitudes to unemployment in one LEA were explored by Gothard (1983). 43 secondary schools responded to a questionnaire, sent out a few months before Y.T.S. was launched. It showed that only 35% of schools felt that the Scheme was worthwhile, while 30% saw it merely as a means of occupying time. Nearly half did not have enough information to judge, and 28% saw the Scheme as a device to reduce the unemployment figures. (Percentages add up to more than 100% as some schools responded to more than one item). The figures do bring out two points. Firstly, the lack of information about Y.T.S. available to schools, and secondly, the scepticism of some schools about the reasons for establishing the Y.T.S. Schools were in the vast majority of cases dealing with the topic of unemployment in a variety of different ways in careers lessons; nearly all of them referring to Y.T.S. at some point. Unemployment only formed an important part of careers education in 23% of schools, which is not surprising as it was still not a severe problem in the area surveyed. This was borne out by the fact that 63% of schools were fairly optimistic about the employment prospects of its pupils.

It is necessary to make a number of points about the nature of some sorts of work before concluding this discussion of unemployment. The understandable concentration of attention upon youth unemployment can mask the very unsatisfactory nature of many of the jobs done by young people. These jobs offer little or no training, few prospects of advancement, little interest and fewer and fewer opportunities to acquire skills. Work can also be dangerous at times, and many jobs are structured in such a way that employees are dominated by the machinery with which they work, and can become "dehumanised". This is another side of the "unacceptable face" of capitalism. The option of such a job, or unemployment, may make the latter a more acceptable alternative to many youngsters.

Special Programmes - Y.O.P. and Y.T.S.

The Manpower Services Commission (MSC) set up a committee chaired by Geoffrey Holland in 1976 to investigate the feasibility of guaranteeing every youngster between 16-18 a job, education or training. The resulting report in 1977 proposed a Youth Opportunities Programme (YOP) which was established in 1978. The Holland Report argued that the least able and least qualified were most in need of help, so Y.O.P. began as essentially a 'shield' for this disadvantaged group. It was also seen as providing some skill training, as a possible access to job-getting networks, as a means of work orientation, as a surrogate further education course, and as an important setting for social integration and support (P.Jones et al 1983).

Y.O.P. was made up of various different schemes and the number of entrants onto these schemes is shown in Table 2. (The total number of youngsters on Y.O.P. fell in 1982/3 to 543,100).

Table 8.2 Y.O.P.distribution of entrants by scheme type 1981/2 (Source SPD)

Work Experience on Employers Premises		%
(WEEP)	371,200	67
Community Projects (CP)	74,100	13
Training Workshops (TW)	16,200	3
Total Work Experience	461,500	83
Employment Induction Courses (EIC)	3,700	1
Short Training Course (STC)	85,800	15
Remedial Courses (RC)	2,000	1
Total Work Preparation	91,500	17
TOTAL	553,000	100

WEEP gave youngsters the opportunity to work alongside the sponsor's workforce and discover what the job was all about. Training workshops provided training and experience in labour intensive, productive environments, and Community projects provided young people with the opportunity to do things of value for the community. Work preparation schemes were run by Colleges of Further Education.

Y.O.P. developed rapidly from 162,200 entrants in 1978/9 to 553,000 entrants in 1981/2. A national sample of over 3,000 young people who joined Y.O.P. in 1978/9 were interviewed a year after leaving a scheme (Bedeman and Harvey 1981). Some 30% were given no information prior to joining a scheme, and about half were also given no information about safety at work when they joined a scheme. Only about 20% were given any guidance on job seeking, whilst less than a third were contacted on a scheme by the Careers Service. Overall attitudes to Y.O.P. were very favourable, especially in respect of the trainee's self confidence, and helping them to get on with other people. Nearly half enjoyed the work they did, especially those on a Community Scheme. Immediately on leaving a scheme, 48% went directly into a job. Six months after leaving, 60% were in a job, 19% unemployed, 14% on another Y.O.P. scheme, 3% in education and 5% not seeking work.

Another study of 565 boys and girls leaving school in 1979 concentrated on leavers from 6 comprehensive schools in an area of Birmingham (P Jones et al 1983). They were interviewed at least twice over a two year period. A total of 108 youngsters entered Y.O.P.; girls, those of West Indian origins, youngsters with no qualifications and those in ill-health were over-represented on schemes. Overall, 60% of Y.O.P. trainees held predominantly positive attitudes to the scheme. Those critical of the schemes mentioned poor training and low wages in particular. Being on a Y.O.P. scheme seemed to make little difference to the youngster's chance of getting a job (with the exception of a small group of unqualified white boys). Y.O.P. helped very few of those of West Indian origin to get jobs. As the study says

> "Y.O.P. had only limited success in compensating for inequalities of social background or inequalities in the labour market. In many respects it reflected the pattern of opportunities already available to young people".

Y.O.P. came in for a good deal of critical comment during its fairly brief history, which is not surprising bearing in mind that over 100,000 sponsors were involved in the programme in 1982 alone. Criticisms ranged from poor training to the exploitation of cheap young labour, and no doubt some of this was true. Certainly, there were a disturbing number of accidents at work involving Y.O.P. trainees. As regards Y.O.P. experience leading to an actual job, the figures show a steady decline in the number actually finding work. In 1978, 3/4 were employed, or were in education and training at the end of Y.O.P. In 1982, this figure was down to 52%. A lack of satisfaction with Y.O.P. contributed to the introduction of the Youth Training Scheme.

Before considering Y.T.S., mention must be made of other initiatives that have developed in response to the growing problem of youth unemployment. Although the MSC schemes deal with the vast majority of unemployed youngsters, there are a number of interesting schemes which have not been initiated by the MSC. Instant Muscle is one of these schemes, which a number of leading firms fund, and which was begun in 1981 by a management consultant, Peter Raynes. It has helped establish some 24 cooperatives, totalling about 200 youngsters. Instant Muscle aim to help young people to start cooperatives, which do a wide variety of jobs such as lawn cutting, required by the local community. The philosophy behind the scheme rests upon a belief that young people have an entrepreneurial streak, that needs initial encouragement. Project Fullemploy dates back to 1976, and has been particularly successful in helping young blacks. Funded by the MSC and business, it has 10 training centres, dealing with 1,000 youngsters in 1982, and has had a high rate of success in finding jobs for its trainees. The MSC are keen to promote 'self help' schemes, particularly amongst the black community.

The Youth Training Scheme was begun in 1983, funded by a Government grant of £1 billion and planned to provide places for 460,000 young people. Y.T.S. grew out of the 'New Training Initiative', published in 1981, which set out the following objectives; reform of skill training, including apprenticeship, development of comprehensive vocational preparation for young people under 18, and the opening up of wider opportunities for adults to train and re-train. The one year scheme is designed for all abilities and will combine training, planned work experience and further education.

Y.T.S. will aim to impart basic skills, and provide trainees with a knowledge of the world of work. It has the objective of imparting skills that can be transferred between jobs. Finally, there is an emphasis on trainees developing themselves more broadly, as members of the community, and becoming more self reliant. The following design element have been defined:

1.) Induction - should be planned to meet trainees needs.

2.) Occupationally based training - learning skills related to a broad group of occupations.

3.) Off the job training/education - 13 weeks, which could take place at college or employers premises on day or block release basis.

4.) Planned work experience - learning by doing, but systematically planned.

5.) Core areas - this covers number and its application, communication, problem solving and planning, manual/practical skills and computer literacy.

6.) Guidance and support - each trainee will have a named person, within the scheme, who will review the trainee's progress, on a regular and personal basis.

7.)Assessment - initial assessment within the first 4 weeks, followed by further assessments.

8.)Review and recording of progress achievement and certification - systematic review and recording should take place, and all trainees will receive a certificate, at the end of the Scheme.

YTS programmes are run by a sponsor who can be an employer, local authority, college or voluntary organisation. Most schemes have to be approved by the local MSC; final approval being made by the Area Manpower Board. This Board is made up of representatives from employers, trade unions, the Careers Service, Further education, elected representatives and Chief Education Officers.

Schemes are either Mode A or Mode B. Mode A schemes are for the employed and unemployed, and are employer based. Each scheme has a 'managing agent' who is responsible for the whole 12 month programme. Something in the region of 70% of all YTS schemes are Mode A. It is important to note that some YTS trainees are actually employees who are spending their first year of employment in the scheme. They are funded by the MSC on an additionality basis, i.e. two employed trainees for three extra unemployed trainees.

Mode B is for the unemployed, and has two elements. Mode B1 schemes (85,000 trainees) are either in Training Workshops, Information Technology Centres (ITEC) or Community Projects.

Training Workshops may be sponsored by any responsible organisation, typically a local authority, and produce goods or provide services, as far as possible, on a commercial basis. Their main objective, however, is to train youngsters in adaptable skills. ITEC's specialise in new technologies such as computer programming, tele-text editing, word processing, computer maintenance, digital techniques, control systems and electronics. Each centre normally provides 30 places. Community projects featured largely in YOP and will continue in YTS. Typically, they may provide leisure facilities for the public, care for the old and handicapped, or help run play groups. A large project might offer up to 200 places. Mode B2 are called 'linked schemes' (80,000 trainees). Unlike B1 schemes, they rely on employers for planned work experience. They are designed to be flexible, so they might offer longer than 13 weeks off the job training, for example. "Low achievers" may well enter such schemes, which will include experience with a number of employers.

YTS is expected to become the 'normal' entry to work for all 16 year olds in the future, providing a training 'bridge' from school to work. It is not compulsory, although those not accepting a place may ultimately have their benefit reduced. A trainee will be able to leave a scheme and possibly move to another scheme. By the autumn of 1983, the take up places on YTS schemes had been slow, although there were still hopes that by the end of the year, numbers would have risen considerably. The apparent lack of enthusiasm for the scheme could be due to limited publicity, poor image of YOP, lowish YTS allowance of £25 per week etc.

Ultimately, too many YTS places may have been offered in this first trial year; particularly in some areas, where there are still jobs for youngsters. In one LEA, the Young Worker scheme has been used by some employers in preference to YTS. In this instance, an employer can get a government subsidy without having to go to the trouble of complying with YTS requirements. YTS was rushed into existence and this has presented great problems to schools, the Careers Service, parents and youngsters, who have mostly had inadequate information about schemes. In some instances, youngsters have been getting 'real' jobs which they have taken in preference to YTS, whist others have opted to stay at school. There has certainly been a problem in some areas of getting the right balance of schemes available, whilst not enough emphasis has been given to getting employers to take employees on to YTS as well as the unemployed. Some success has been achieved in merging first year apprenticeship training into YTS in Agriculture and Construction, and this process is likely to continue in other industries, within the next few years.

It is too early to judge the success of the Youth Training Scheme. As the YTS has been rushed into existence, there will certainly be problems and failures in the first year. However, the Government and the MSC are heavily committed to YTS and it will certainly continue for some years to come, although some modifications are likely. However, good the scheme is, its credibility, to a large extent, will depend on how many trainees get permanent jobs at the end of the scheme. In a sense, this 'test' of the scheme is not fair as the state of the economy is not linked to it, but in the eyes of most youngsters, YTS is about getting a job. Bearing in mind the depressed state of Britain's economy, the prospect for YTS trainees in 1984 is not encouraging.

The intention is to extend YTS provision to those over 17, as well, from 1984 onwards. Before the end of this decade, it is possible that all youngster who leave school at 16 will spend their first and possibly their second year in some version of YTS. This may, in fact, be the only way of providing this groups with some sort of "work". However, no one pretends that the scheme will provide a permanent solution to the problems of youth unemployment. Large numbers of jobs need to be created by some source in the next few years to absorb the many youngsters leaving school and YTS. Those working in vocational guidance will continue to be confronted by this harsh reality.

Occupational Training Families (OTF) are a concept of considerable importance to YTS. This concept has been developed by Hayes and Fonda of the Institute of Manpower Studies for MSC, and arose out of three "key benefits" arising from YTS. These benefits for YTS trainees were defined as firstly, competence which comes from being able to do a 'real' job, secondly, "ownership" of skills and knowledge, and finally, ability to redeploy skills and knowledge in unfamiliar situations.

By defining eleven OTFs, Hayes and Fonda (1983) have provided a structure for looking at jobs and identifyng their key purposes and the competencies essential to achieve these purposes. Not all jobs fit into these 'families', but it is claimed that the vast majority of jobs for sixteen-year olds do.

Table 8.3 Occupational Training Families and their key purposes

OTF	Key Purpose
1.) Administrative, clerical and office services	Information processing
2.) Agriculture, horticulture forestry and fisheries	Nurturing and gathering living resources.
3.) Craft and design	Creating single or small numbers of objects using hand or power tools.
4.) Installing, maintenance and repair	Applying known procedures for making equipment work
5.) Technical and scientific	Applying known principles to making things work or usable.
6.) Manufacturing and Assembly	Transforming metallic and non-metallic materials through shaping, constructing and assembling into products.
7.) Processing	Intervening in the working of machines when necessary.
8.) Food preparation and service	Transform and handle edible matter.

9.) Personal service and sales.	Satisfying the needs of individual customers.
10.) Community and Health Services.	Meeting socially defined needs of the community.
11.) Transport Services	Moving goods and people.

The OTF work learning guide uses a chart for each family to show what a trainee should be able to do, and the relevance of each competence. This is helpful to both trainee and trainer in identifying training objectives and seeing how they relate.

Technical and Vocational Education Initiative TVEI

It is appropriate to mention TVEI, having discussed YTS. TVEI is a 5 year pilot scheme, funded by the Government to stimulate the provision of technical and vocational education for 14-18 year olds in the education system. In 1983/4, some 14 LEAs will be operating pilot projects for the first time. The projects adopt different approaches, but all are within national criteria and guidelines. They all offer a 4 year course starting at 14, of full time general, technical and vocational education, including work experience, for youngsters of all abilities. They will all lead to nationally recognised qualifications and are run in existing schools and colleges. Finally, they are all optional. Each project has about 250 pupils initially, reaching a maximum of 1,000 at the end of the project. The MSC are aiming to include further LEAs in the scheme in 1984.

TVEI reflects a dissatisfaction by the Government with the quality of technical and vocational education in schools. It can be seen as a radical change of emphasis, with the infusion of MSC funds into the secondary education system. A National Steering group has been established to advise the MSC, and to produce national criteria and guidelines. It draws its membership from education and industry. The national criteria are broad, and it is intended that projects should be managed locally, and the curriculum should also be determined locally. It is worth noting that it is suggested that teachers and instructors from industry may be necessary to ensure that projects have the correct expertise.

The national criteria state that "Good careers and educational counselling will be essential". Submissions from LEAs to the MSC have to state the changes or enhancement proposed in guidance and counselling. Likewise, it is gratifying to see that "care should be taken to avoid sex stereotyping". TVEI is breaking controversial ground by involving the MSC in secondary education, especially at a time when the Government is cutting back on expenditure in all areas of education. The initiative reflects a tacit agreement with the dissatisfaction of many employers, who have been consistently critical of much of secondary education. It could be the beginning of a major change in the nature and control of the curriculum. Equally, many young people would welcome a greater "relevance" to their school work and TVEI may supply this. On the other hand, it could be interpreted, in the words of one headteacher, as "divisive", with one group being hived off at 14 to follow a 'narrow' technical route, which could be seen both as second class and too early a stage to specialise. Finally, it is worth quoting Geoffrey Holland's comments about TVEI. He makes the important point about values and education, suggesting that these have to be changed in order to give the Initiative a real chance of succeeding. This will inevitably take a long time.

The future of Vocational Guidance

"I think there is now a real requirement of the Careers Service to re-think its role".

These are the words of Geoffrey Holland, Director of MSC (1983). Holland sees YTS as signalling a need for a radical change in careers education and advice, with young people initially thinking more in terms of 'occupational training families' and less in terms of individual jobs. He suggests that the Career Service has laid too much emphasis on guidance and counselling, and too little on placement with the result that employers have become "alienated" from the Service. This suggestion is hard to accept, bearing in mind the almost total lack of opportunity to place young people in jobs in some areas of Britain. However, while Holland's remarks are unfair to most of the Careers Service, his views do signify a new challenge to the Service.

These views have been more forcefully expressed by an Employment Minister, Peter Morrison, early in 1983. He is quoted as saying that

> "the best way to help young people get jobs and training is to act with market forces, not against them. Employers are operating in the real world - the world of profits. The Careers Service must respond positively to the indications employers give about the sort of youngster they want".

The implication behind these comments is that the Careers Service best helps young people by serving the interests of employers, who represent the "real world". This view would be shared by some in the Careers Service, but it deserves close examination.

Employers can in fact be seen as "failing" to employ and to train youngsters in sufficient numbers, hence the need for £1 billion YTS. Perhaps the "real world of profits" does not permit the widespread employment and the adequate training of young people? The Careers Service has always occupied an uneasy, sometimes uncomfortable but essential middle ground between employers, education, parents and young people. It is based within the Education Service, unlike the MSC, and has always subscribed to a philosophy of caring for individual youngsters, first and foremost. The Careers Service, unlike the Jobcentres, exists to help youngsters, rather than to fill employers' vacancies.

The Careers Service must be closely involved with YTS at all stages. Initially, it should play the leading role in facilitating the movement of young people from school to the scheme. Once on YTS, youngsters must be able to consult their Careers Officer and use him or her as an impartial adviser about both the scheme and their future jobs. The Careers Service is the key institution for helping youngsters use YTS to their advantage. However good the guidance offered by the scheme's sponsors, the Careers Service must be able to keep in touch with youngsters, at all stages.

This will put a considerable strain on Career Services resources, but it is a priority. Increasingly, Careers Officers are not interviewing all school leavers individually, and are reducing the amount of time spent in schools. Rightly or wrongly, this is likely to continue. This increases the need for good Careers Education supplied by the school. Careers teachers are still not trained sufficiently well, they continue to have too little time allocated to their role and they have too few resources. Computer based guidance systems offer some hope of improving the quality of information and help offered to pupils. Systems such as JIIG-CAL seem likely to increase and, sensibly deployed, can be very valuable additions to the other resources available.

Vocational guidance needs to be brought much more into the mainstream of guidance work done in the school. There are signs that this is happening in the context of social education, lifeskills teaching and Active Tutorial Work. Youngsters need to be helped to cope with the difficult world they will face outside school. In particular, Careers staff must play a more active role in altering stereotypes that serve to limit the opportunities open to black youngsters and to many girls. The lack of available paid employment is no reason for Careers staff to be seen as irrelevant. Indeed, their role, as counsellors, becomes all the more important in such a stressful context. Many youngsters are very vulnerable in the first few years of leaving school and they need a sympathetic, well informed and impartial person who is available to talk to about a range of personal, vocational and educational matters.

BIBLIOGRAPHY

ALLEN S. and SMITH C.R., (1975) in BRANNEN P. (ed) '<u>Entering the World of Work</u>'. H.M.S.O., London

ARCHER J. and LLOYD B. (1983) '<u>Sex and Gender</u>'. Penguin, London.

ARGYLE M. (1975) '<u>Bodily Communication</u>'. Methuen, London.

ASHTON D.N., MAGUIRE M.J. and GARLAND V. (1982) '<u>Youth in the Labour Market</u>'. Dept. of Employment Research Paper 34.

BALDWIN J. and WELLS H. (1981) '<u>Active Tutorial Work</u>'. Basil Blackwell, Oxford.

BANNISTER D. and FRANSELLA F. (1977) '<u>Inquiring Man</u>'. Penguin, London.

BARRY R. and WOLF B. (1962) '<u>Epitaph for Vocational Guidance</u>'. Columbia University, U.S.A.

BARTON L. and WALKER S. (1983) '<u>Race, Class and Education'. Croom Helm, London.</u>

BEDEMAN T. and HARVEY J. (1981) '<u>Young People on Y.O.P.</u>'. M.S.C. Sheffield.

BENETT Y. and CARTER D. (1981) '<u>Sidetracked?</u>' A look at the Careers Advice given to 5th form girls. E.O.C.

BENJAMIN A (1969) '<u>The Helping Interview</u>' Houghton Mifflin, U.S.A.

BLAV P.M. et al. (1956) '<u>Occupational Choice - a conceptual framework</u>'. Industrial and Labour Review 9.

BOLLES R.N. (1979) '<u>The Quick Job Hunting Map</u>'. Ten Speed Press, California.

BORDIN E.S. et al (1963) '<u>An Articulated Framework for Vocational Development</u>'. Journal of Counselling Psychology, 10.

BOROW H. ed (1973) '<u>Career Guidance for a New Age</u>' Houghton Mifflin, U.S.A.

BOWLES S. & GINTIS H. (1976) '<u>Schooling in Capitalist America</u>'. Routledge, Kegan Paul, London.

BRANNEN P. (1975) '<u>Entering the World of Work</u>' H.M.S.O., London.

BRENTALL D.J. (1981) '<u>Career Guidance and the Vocational Preference Inventory</u>'. Careers Quarterly.

BROWNE M. (1981) '<u>Careers Opportunities and Education</u>' E.O.C.

BUTLER J.R. (1968) '<u>Occupational Choice</u>'. H.M.S.O., London.

CAMPBELL D.P. (1977) '<u>Manual for the Strong Campbell Interest Inventory</u>'. 2nd Edition, Stanford University Press, California.

CASSON M. (1979) '<u>Youth Unemployment</u>'. Macmillan, London.

CHAMBERLAIN P.J. (1982) '<u>Careers Lessons and Careers Awareness of 5th Form Students</u>'. British Journal of Guidance and Counselling 10,1.

CLARKE L. (1980) '<u>Occupational Choice</u>'. H.M.S.O., London.

CLARKE L. (1980) '<u>The Practice of Vocational Guidance</u>'. H.M.S.O., London.

CLARKE L. (1980) '<u>The Transition from School to Work</u>'. H.M.S.O., London.

CLEATON D. and FOSTER R. (1981) '<u>Practical Aspects of Guidance - Careers Education</u>'. Careers Consultants, London.

CLOSS S.J. (1981) '<u>Manual for JIIG-CAL System</u>'. Edinburgh.

COLLINS. R. (1972) in '<u>Education: Structure and Society</u>'. ed. B.R. COSIN, Penguin, London.

COSIN B.R. (1972) '<u>Education: Structure and Society</u>'. Penguin, London.

CRITES J.O. (1969) 'Vocational Psychology'. McGraw Hill, New York.

CURRAGH E.F. and McGLEENAN C.F. (1980) 'A systematic approach to planning a Careers Education Course'. British Journal of Guidance and Counselling 8,1.

DAUNCEY G. (1982) 'The Unemployment Handbook'. National Extension College, London.

DAWS P.P. (1972) 'A Good Start in Life'. CRAC, London

DAWS P.P. (1977) 'Are Careers Education Programmes in secondary schools a waste of time?'. British Journal of Guidance and Counselling 5,1.

DEPT. OF EDUCATION AND SCIENCE (1973) 'Careers Education in Secondary Schools'. Survey 18 H.M.S.O., London.

DEPT. OF EDUCATION AND SCIENCE (1981) 'Schools and Working Life'. H.M.S.O., London.

DEPT. OF EMPLOYMENT (1981) 'Computer Applications in the Careers Service'. Careers Service Branch.

ECOLOGY PARTY (1981) 'Working for a Future'. Ecology Party, London.

EGAN G. (1982) 'Skilled Helping'. Brooks/Cole, U.S.A.

EGGLESTON J. (1982) 'Work Experience in Secondary Schools'. Routledge, Kegan and Paul, London.

EMPLOYMENT SERVICES AGENCY (1975) 'The D.E.V.A.T. Manual'.

EQUAL OPPORTUNITIES COMMISSION (1980) 'Breakthrough' E.O.C.

FITZGERALD L.F. and CRITES J.O. (1980) 'Towards a Career Psychology of Women'. Journal of Counselling Psychology.

FLEMING D. and LAVERCOMBE S. (1982) 'Talking about Unemployment with School Leavers'. British Journal of Guidance and Counselling 10,1.

FOGELMAN K. (1979) 'Educational and Career Aspirations of Sixteen Year Olds'. British Journal of Guidance and Counselling Vol 7. No.1.

FURTHER EDUCATION UNIT (1983) 'Supporting Y.T.S.'. F.E.U., U.K.

FURTHER EDUCATION UNIT (1983) 'Towards a Personal Guidance Base'. F.E.U., U.K.

GELATT H.B. (1962) 'Decision-making:A conceptual frame of reference for counselling'. Journal of Counselling Psychology. 9.1962.

GINZBERG E. et al (1951) 'Occupational Choice'. Columbia University Press, New York.

GOLDMAN L. (1971) 'Using Tests in Counselling'. Appleton Century Crafts, U.S.A.

GOTHARD W.P. (1982) 'The Brightest and the Best'. Nafferton Press, Yorkshire.

GOTHARD W.P. (1983) 'Schools and Unemployment'. Paper in Preparation.

GROSS E. (1958) 'Work and Society'. Thomas Y Crowell Co.

HALSEY A.H. (1981) 'Change in British Society'. Oxford University Press.

HANSEN L.S. (1979) Counseling and Career (Self) Development of Women in Peters and Hansen 'Vocational Guidance and Career Development'. Mcgraw Hill, U.S.A.

HAYES J. (1971) 'Occupational Perceptions and Occupational Information'. Institute of Careers Officers, U.K.

HEGINBOTHAM H. (1951) 'The Youth Employment Service'. Methuen, U.K.

HOLDSWORTH R. (1976) 'Using Tests in Vocational Guidance'. Institute of Careers Officers. U.K.

HOLDSWORTH R. (1982) 'Psychology for Careers Counselling'. Macmillan, London.

HOLLAND G. (1983) 'Interview with Geoffrey Holland'. Newscheck 1,1

HOLLAND J.L. (1966) 'Psychology of Vocational Choice'. Blaisdell, U.S.A.

HOLLAND J.L. (1973) 'Making Vocational Choices'. Prentice Hall, U.S.A.

HOLLAND J.L. (1977) 'The Self Directed Search and Occupations Finder'. Consulting Psychologists Press, U.S.A.

HOLLAND J.L. & GOTTFRIEDSON G.D. (1976) 'Using an typology of persons and environments to explain careers'. The Counseling Psychologist 6,3.

HOLLAND J.L. (1978) 'Vocational Preference Inventory Manual'. Consulting Psychologists Press, U.S.A.

HOPSON B. & HAYES J. (1968) 'The Theory and Practice of Vocational Guidance'. Pergamon, U.K.

HOPSON B. & HOUGH P. (1973) 'Exercises in Personal and Career Development'. CRAC, U.K.

HOPSON B. & SCALLY M. (198?) 'Life Skills Manual 1 & 2'.

HUDSON L. (1968) 'Frames of Mind'. Penguin, London

HUNT E.P. & SMITH P. (1944) 'Scientific Vocational Guidance and its Value to the Choice of Employment'. City of Birmingham Education Committee.

ILLICH I. (1978) 'The Right to Useful Unemployment'. M. Boyars, U.K.

JAHODA M. (1982) 'Employment and Unemployment'. Cambridge University Press.

JAMIESON I. & LIGHTFOOT M. (1982) 'Schools and Industry'. Methuen, London.

JONES A., MARSH J. & WATTS A.G. (1974) 'Male and Female'. CRAC, Cambridge.

JONES J.E.M. (1983) 'The uses employers make of

examinaton results and other tests for selection and employment'. University of Reading.

JONES P. et al (1983) 'Out of School' M.S.C. S.P. Paper No.4, Sheffield.

KELLY A. et al (1982) 'Gender Roles at Home and School'. British Journal of Sociology of Education, Vol.3, No.3.

KELLY G. (1955) 'A Theory of Personality'. Norton, N. York.

KELSALL K. et al (1972) 'Graduates, the Sociology of an Elite'. Methuen, London.

KING J.S. (1974) 'Women and Work'. H.M.S.O. London.

KIRTON M. (1976) 'Career Knowledge of 6th form Boys'. C.O.I.C. U.K.

KIRTON M. (1979) 'Career Information, a Job Knowledge Index'. Heineman Education, London.

KLINE P. (1975) 'Psychology of Vocational Guidance'. Batsford, London.

KNASEL E. et al (1982) 'The Benefit of Experience'. M.S.C. Research and Development Series No.5.

KOWALCZEWSKI P.S. (1982) 'Race and Education'. Oxford Review of Education 8,2.

KRUMBOLTZ J. (1976) 'A Social Learning Theory of Career Selection'. The Counselling Psychologist 6,1.

LANCASHIRE R. & HOLDSWORTH R. (1976) 'Career Change'. Hobsons Press, London.

LAW W. (1981) in WATTS A.G. et al 'Career Development in Britain'. Hobsons Press, London.

LAW W. (1981) 'Careers Education and Curriculum Priorities in Secondary Schools'. Educational Analysis 3,2.

McGUIRE & PRIESTLEY P.(1981) 'Life after School'. Pergamon, U.K.

McROBBIE A. & McCABE T. (1981) '<u>Feminism for Girls</u>' Routledge, Kegan Paul, London.

MANPOWER SERVICES COMMISSION (1983) '<u>Occupational Training Families</u>'. M.S.C./I.M.S.

MASLOW A.H. (1954) '<u>Motivation and Personality</u>'. Harper and Row, New York.

MILLER R. (1981) '<u>Equal Opportunities</u>'. Penguin, London.

MITCHELL A., JONES G.B. & GRUMBOLTZ J. (ed) (1979) '<u>Social Learning and Career Decision Making</u>'. Carroll Press, U.S.A.

MOREA P.C. (1972) '<u>Guidance, Selection and Training</u>'. Routledge, Kegan and Paul, London.

MORGAN J.I. & SKOVHOLT T.M. (1977) '<u>Using inner experience - Fantasy and Daydreams in Career Counselling</u>'. Journal of Counselling Psychology 5.

MUNRO E.A., MANTHEI J. & SMALL J.J. (1983) '<u>Counselling, a skills approach</u>'. Methuen, New Zealand.

MURRAY C. (1978) '<u>Youth Unemployment</u>'. N.F.E.R., Slough.

NATIONAL CONFERENCE REPORT. (1982) '<u>Non Sexist Practice in the Careers Service - Making it Work</u>'.

NELSON-JONES R. (1982) '<u>The Theory and Practice of Counselling Psychology</u>'. Holt, Rinehart and Winston, London.

NEWSOME A. THORNE B.J., & WYLD K.L. (1975) '<u>Student Counselling in Practice</u>'. Unibooks, London.

NOVARRA V. (1981) '<u>Women's Work, Men's Work</u>'. M. Boyars, London.

OAKLEY A. (1982) '<u>Subject Woman</u>'. Fontana, London.

OPEN UNIVERSITY (1978) '<u>EDUCATION and the Urban Environment</u>'. Oxford University Press, U.K.

OSIPOW S.H. (1973) '<u>Theories of Career</u> Development'. Prentice Hall, U.S.A.

PARSONS F. (1909) 'Choosing a Vocation'. Houghton Miffin. U.S.A.

PEARCE B. & VARNEY E. (1981) 'Trainee Centred Reviewing'. M.S.C. Research Series No.2. Sheffield.

PRICE D.G. (1973) 'Experimental Introduction of DEVAT'. CYEE. Internal Research Paper.

PUMFREY P.D. & SCHOFIELD A. (1982) 'Work Experience and the Career Maturity of 5th Form Pupils'. British Journal of Guidance and Counselling 10,2.

RAFFE D. (1983) 'Employment Instability Among Less Qualified Workers'. British Journal of Guidance and Counselling. 11,1.

RAMPTON REPORT (1981) 'West Indian Children in our Schools'. H.M.S.O., London.

RAUTA I. & HUNT A. (1975) '5th Form Girls and Their Hopes for the Future'. O.P.C.S. H.M.S.O., London.

REDDY H.A. & BRANNIGAN C.R. (1982) 'A Resource Package for Interview Training on Careers Guidance Courses'. L.G.T.B.

REID I. & WORMALD E. (ed) (1982) 'Sex Differences in Britain'. Grant Mcintyre, London.

RICHARDSON K. & SPEARS D. (ed) (1972) 'Race, Culture and Intelligence'. Penguin, London.

RICHARDSON S.A. et al (1965) 'Interviewing'. Basic Books. U.S.A.

ROBERTS K. (1968) 'The Entry into Employment, an Approach Towards a General Theory'. The Sociological Review. 16,2.

ROBERTS K. (1971) 'From School to Work'. David and Charles, Newton Abbot.

ROBERTS K. (1977) 'The Social Conditions, Conseqences and Limitations of Careers Guidance'. British Journal of Guidance and Counselling. 5,1.

ROBERTS K. et al (1982) 'Out of School Youth in High Unemployment Areas'. British Journal of Guidance and Counselling. 10,1.

RODGER A. (1971) 'Seven Point Plan'. N.I.I.P.

ROE A. (1956) 'The Psychology of Occupations'. John Wiley, U.S.A.

ROGERS C. (1978) 'Personal Power'. Constable, London.

ROSE M. (1978) 'Industrial Behaviour'. Penguin, London.

ROSS P. (1981) 'The Use of Hypnotic Imagery in Vocational Counselling'. Bulletin of the British Society of Experimental and Clinical Hypnosis.

RUTTER M. & MADGE N. (1977) 'Cycles of Disadvantage'. Heinemann, London.

RYRIE A.C. (1981) 'Schools and Socialization into Work'. Educational Analysis 3,2.

SCHARFF D.E. & HILL J.M.M. (1976) 'Between Two Worlds'. Career Consultants, London.

SCHOOLS COUNCIL (1975) 'Geography Project 14-16'. Longmans, London.

SCHOOLS COUNCIL (1979) 'Careers Education Project - Work 1,2,3'. Longmans, London.

SCOTT F. (1980) 'A Career Interview Planning System for 5th Year Pupils'. Careers Bulletin.

SEABROOK J. (1983) 'Unemployment'. Paladin, London.

SHARPE S. (1976) 'Just Like A Girl'. Pelican, London.

SINFIELD A. (1981) 'What Unemployment Means'. Martin Robertson, London.

SMITH M., HARTLEY J. & STEWART B. (1978) 'A Case Study of Reportory Grids used in Vocational Guidance'. Journal of Occupational Psychology 51.

SPENDER D., & SARAH E. (1980) 'Learning to Lose'. Women's Press, London.

STONE M. (1981) 'The Education of the Black Child in Britain'. Fontana, London.

STORES R., IMBREY D. & McROBIE J. (1982) 'Ethnic Minorities and M.S.C. Special Programmes'. M.S.C. Research Series No.6. Sheffield.

SUPER D.E. & BOHN M.J. (1973) 'Occupational Psychology'. Tavistock, London.

SUPER D. in WATTS A.G. et al (1981) 'Career Development in Britain'. Hobsons Press, London.

SUPER D. (1957) 'The Psychology of Careers'. Harper Row, N. York.

THOMAS R. & WEATHERALL D. (1974) 'Looking Forward to Work'. H.M.S.O., London.

TIEDEMAN D.V. & O'HARA R.P. (1963) 'Career Development'. College Entrance Exam Board, N. York.

TOLBERT E.L. (1974) 'Counselling for Career Development'. Houghton Mifflin, U.S.A.

VAUGHAN T.D. (ed) (1975) 'Concepts of Counselling'. Bedford Square Press, London.

WALKER A. (1982) 'Unqualified and Underemployed'. Macmillan, London.

WARNATH C.F. (1979) in 'Career Counselling'. S.G. Weinrach. McGraw Hill, New York.

WATTS A.G. & HERR E.L. (1976) 'Career(s) Education in Britain and the U.S.A.'. British Journal of Guidance and Counselling 4,2.

WATTS A.G. & KIDD J.M. (1978) 'Evaluating the Effectiveness of Careers Guidance'. Journal of Occupational Psychology, 51.

WATTS A.G. & BALLANTINE M. (1981) 'Computers in Careers Guidance - an overview'. Careers Quarterly.

WATTS A.G., SUPER D.E. & KIDD J.M. (Ed) (1981) 'Career Development in Britain'. Hobsons Press, London.

WATTS A.G. (ed) (1983) 'Work Experience and Schools'. Heinemann, London.

WEINRACH P. (1979) 'Ethnicity and Adolescent

Identity Conflicts in KHAN V.S. (ed) 'Minority Families in Britain'. MacMillan, London.

WEINRACH S.G. (1979) 'Career Counselling'. McGraw Hill, U.S.A.

WELFORD A et al. (ed) (1968) 'Society - Psychological Problems and Methods of Study'. Routledge, Kegan Paul, London.

WEST J. (ed) (1982) 'Work, Women and the Labour Market'. Routledge, Kegan Paul, London.

WEST M. & NEWTON P. (1983) 'The Transition from School to Work'. Croom Helm, London.

WICKS R.P. in HOLDSWORTH R. (1982) 'Psychology for Careers Counselling'. MacMillan, London.

WILLIAMS W.M. (ed) (1974) 'Occupational Choice'. Allen and Unwin, London.

WILLIAMSON E.G. (1965) 'Vocational Counselling'. McGraw Hill, U.S.A.

WILLIS P. (1977) 'Learning to Labour'. Saxon House, London.

WOOLER S. & LEWIS B. (1982) 'Computer Assisted Careers Counselling - a new approach'. British Journal of Guidance and Counselling 10,2.

YOUTHAID (1979) 'Study of the Transition from School to Working Life'. Youthaid, London.

INDEX